How Your Corps Can Grow

The Salvation Army and Church Growth

John Larsson

International Headquarters of The Salvation Army
101 Queen Victoria Street, London EC4P 4EP

Copyright © 1988 The General of The Salvation Army
First published 1988
ISBN O 85412 544 2

COLONEL JOHN LARSSON, BD
became a Salvation Army officer in 1957. He has served
in the British, Scotland and South America West
Territories, and is at present Assistant to the Chief of the
Staff for United Kingdom administrative planning. Prior
to this appointment, he served as training principal at the
International (William Booth Memorial) Training College,
London. The colonel is a well-known composer of
Salvation Army music and is the author of *Doctrine
Without Tears, Spiritual Breakthrough* and *The Man
Perfectly Filled with the Spirit.*

Cover by Jim Moss Graphics

**Printed in Great Britain by
The Campfield Press, St Albans**

Contents

Acknowledgments

In this work which seeks to report on, interpret and apply church growth research to The Salvation Army, my indebtedness to the church growth authors mentioned in the text as well as the many more who are not will be evident on every page.

I would also like to thank all the officers who have so generously shared their material and expertise. In this connection I want to mention Colonel Roy Calvert, Lieut-Colonel Norman Coles and Major Earl McInnes of Canada, Major Dwight Garrington of the USA Central Territory, Major Paul Kellner of the USA Southern Territory, and Major Barry Pobjie of the Australia Eastern Territory. I am especially grateful to Major Rusty S. Adams of the Australia Southern Territory for the resources and counsel provided, and to Auxiliary-Captain Terry Camsey of the USA Western Territory whose I CAN growth strategy I quote and use.

JL

Foreword

The call to 'let God's Army grow' has sounded out from numerous publications over the past decades but it is only in recent years that salvationists have given study in depth to the teaching of the church growth school of research and action.

This call to examine all activities by the measure of their usefulness in furthering spiritual and numerical growth and to use modern methods of investigation and appraisal to achieve objective assessments has won acceptance in a number of territories, where it has been the means of successful growth. However, salvationists have faced the need to translate terms and apply concepts to our own particular tradition and structures.

Colonel John Larsson has performed a valuable service for the Army worldwide by applying church growth insights and disciplines to The Salvation Army situation, spelling them out in our terms and in the light of his considerable knowledge and experience. He has also provided practical guidance on how to aid corps growth.

We are in the colonel's debt and I commend this book to officers and soldiers everywhere for reading, reflection, prayer and action.

We do not 'grow the Army', God does. So with clear goals and a strong prayer life may the Spirit lead us into a new era of faith and vision and fruitfulness. And may God's Army continue to grow.

Eva Burrows.

General

1
Introducing church growth

The Salvation Army did not begin with a big bang. By early 1878, after 13 years of plodding growth as The Christian Mission, it had only 30 stations and 36 evangelists to show for its labours.

But in 1878 came the dramatic change of name to The Salvation Army. 'From that moment,' wrote W. T. Stead, 'its destiny was fixed—the whole organisation was dominated by the name.' New strategies to match the inspiration of its name were devised with breath-taking speed. Old methods were discarded or adapted and new ones invented. 'An irresistible spiritual offensive swept over cities, towns and villages in every direction, and set the whole country ablaze,' writes Robert Sandall. The results were spectacular by any standard. By the end of the year the number of stations had doubled and the number of evangelists had trebled. By 1886, eight years later, there were 1,006 corps in Britain and 2,260 officers—a growth rate of 3,300 per cent and 6,200 per cent respectively!

How does one account for such startling growth? It would be too simplistic to say that it was all due to God sending a revival. Any explanation which seeks to ascribe the growth solely to more spiritual power being available after 1878 than in the previous 13 years must be incomplete. Full justice can only be done to the facts by

1

including the sweeping changes in style and tactics which flowed from the change of name. William Booth took hold of the exciting possibilities inherent in the new title and, with the experience of nearly 30 years as an evangelist, forged his mission into an effective army of salvation. The near-miraculous outcome was as much due to these God-inspired changes of methods and strategies as to any increase in divine revival power.

In recent years such examples of rapid expansion have been subjected to careful study with the object of seeking to draw from them any principles of growth that might have application in other places and at other times. With the intuition and skill of the evangelistic genius he was, William Booth in fact incorporated into the concept of The Salvation Army a whole host of such principles—principles which are now recognised as basic to any church wishing to fulfil its evangelistic mission. Among such church growth principles evident in the early day Salvation Army and its expansion can be mentioned:

☐ Expectancy of growth. The early day salvationists meant what they said about winning the world for Jesus!

☐ Strong leadership. Church growth research today confirms that committee-led churches are less likely to grow than those where the leadership is vested in the minister.

☐ Leadership and membership committed to growth and willing to pay the price. In the early Salvation Army there simply was no other aim but effective evangelism.

☐ Pragmatic approach to evangelistic strategy. When it came to evangelistic methods, William Booth believed in what worked.

☐ No need for newcomers and new converts to cross class or cultural barriers. Everything, from the style of worship to the 'neutral' buildings often employed, was designed to make people feel at ease.

☐ Emphasis on converts becoming members. In church growth language, the aim was not only 'decisions' but 'disciples'. In Salvation Army terminology, the objective was to turn each new convert into a fighting soldier.

☐ Effective assimilation of new members. Corps life was geared to this. Adding new soldiers to the ranks was a continuous process.

☐ Total mobilisation of the membership, each according to his ability. There was a task for everyone in the Army, and the idea of non-combatant soldiers would have seemed a contradiction in terms.

With such basic principles of growth built into its structure it is no surprise that The Salvation Army not only grew rapidly in the country of its origin, but that it soon leapt national boundaries and became an international movement that has been growing ever since.

In some countries, however, the growth of the church as a whole has been arrested for a variety of reasons, and The Salvation Army has not always been exempt from the national trend. What the church growth movement is saying to all churches, including the Army, today is that such situations need not be permanent. Decline is not inevitable. Church growth research is enabling the Church to diagnose and remove obstacles to growth. The church growth movement has therefore something important to say to The Salvation Army.

THE CHURCH GROWTH MOVEMENT

Church growth research began in the 1930s on the mission field. Dr Donald A. McGavran, an American missionary serving in India, became disturbed by the small increase in church membership they were seeing despite the vast resources in money and personnel being invested, and began to ask searching questions.

Why do some churches grow, while others in a similar context do not? Why do some parts of the Church grow while other parts do not? The study of church growth had begun.

It was not until many years later, however, that the spark was to burst into flames. In 1955 McGavran

3

published his book *Bridges of God*, and in 1960 he founded the Institute of Church Growth in Eugene, Oregon. The church growth movement traces its origin to one or the other of these events.

In 1965 McGavran became the founding dean of Fuller Seminary's School of World Mission and moved his Institute of Church Growth to Fuller Theological Seminary in Pasadena, California. At the institute case-studies of growing and non-growing churches were researched in the light of biblical teaching in order to seek principles of growth that might have abiding and universal application. This research was mainly centred on the third world. But when, in 1972, Dr McGavran and Dr C. Peter Wagner conducted a pilot course in church growth designed for American church leaders and the American scene, church growth caught fire. The church growth movement became hot news.

A number of developments followed from this. As research at Fuller became increasingly directed to the home scene other significant organisations evolved around it. These included the Institute for American Church Growth (now Church Growth Inc.), the US Centre for World Missions, and the Missions Advanced Research and Communications Centre (MARC), a ministry of the Evangelism and Research Division of World Vision International. The Church Growth Book Club, begun in 1970, added a subsidiary directed to the American scene. *The Global Church Bulletin*, a bi-monthly magazine published by McGavran since 1964, became increasingly influential and was supplemented by *Church Growth: America*, published by the Institute for American Church Growth. A number of other associations, agencies and consultancies were formed, and most main-line denominations started church growth departments of their own in which the research was adapted and applied to their own circumstances.

Researchers from Canada, Britain, Australia and other countries studied at Fuller and returned to continue and apply their research to their national religious scenes. Church growth agencies were created. The Canadian Church Growth Centre was established in Regina,

Saskatchewan, and the publication of *Church Growth Canada* began. The British Church Growth Association was formed in 1981, complementing the pioneering work of the Bible Society which, since 1978, had been spreading church growth teaching throughout Britain. In Australia the Australian Fellowship for Church Growth was commenced. In many countries church growth was added to the curriculum of theological colleges and Bible schools.

An enormous explosion of creative research and publishing has resulted from these developments. There is now a vast body of material in the form of books, bulletins, films, videos and audio-cassettes dealing with church growth. It is continually being added to as principles of growth are applied to different church situations, new principles are discovered, and experiences and insights are exchanged. Among the church growth writers quoted in this book mention should be made of Peter Wagner and Lyle E. Schaller, who are two of the most influential authorities in the USA, and Roy Pointer and Eddie Gibbs, who are recognised British specialists on the subject.

The Salvation Army has not stood back from these developments. The pioneer territory was Canada which, in 1976, established a link with the Fuller Institute. A number of seminars for officers were arranged in that territory, and it became mandatory for divisional commanders to attend the Fuller Institute. A director of church growth was appointed at territorial headquarters and the term 'church growth' became an accepted part of Army terminology. Developments in Canada were watched with interest throughout the Army world. Canadian officers conducted seminars in other countries, including Australia and Britain. Individual officers from other territories enrolled as students at the Fuller Institute and took the fruit of their research back to their respective countries.

Co-ordinators for church growth were next appointed in the two Australian territories. In May 1986 General Jarl Wahlström wrote about church growth to all territorial leaders and officers commanding, and when, later that year, General Eva Burrows assumed the generalship the

5

subject was further highlighted by her forthright declaration that 'the means I hope to use in the development of the Army's evangelistic programmes will be based on church growth principles'. Territorial impetus is now being given to church growth in a number of territories around the world, including, in the English-speaking countries, the British Territory, the four USA territories, the Scotland Territory, the Australian territories and the New Zealand and Fiji Territory. Material of very high quality in photocopied form is being produced by some of these territories.

CHURCH GROWTH THINKING

Church growth is not an organisation, nor is it a set of unalterable dogmas set down once and for all. It is a school of thought, a series of theological assumptions and convictions based on Scripture, an ever-expanding body of research, and an open-ended number of growth principles with wide application drawn from practical experience.

Church growth sees the New Testament as its basic document, written 'from church growth people to church growth people about church growth'. Its modern Magna Carta, to quote Peter Wagner, is Donald McGavran's *Understanding Church Growth* (published by Eerdman in 1971, but completely revised and expanded in 1980). The revised edition, produced by the author at the age of 83, distils the teaching of a lifetime, and will always remain the foundational resource book of the church growth movement.

Numerous writers have since developed and added to the teaching given by the patriarch, but all church growth writing acknowledges its indebtedness to his thinking. However, on a subject so scriptural, and as old as the Early Church, and of so wide and diverse application, no one can claim a monopoly of insights. As Delos Miles puts it, 'there are no denominationally pure streams of church growth in the world. Everybody who wants to do church growth is drinking from everyone else's fountain.' The source of it all, however, remains McGavran's original research, and this is what gives a certain cohesiveness to church growth thinking despite the variety of approach. It is this factor which enables Church Growth to be written with capital letters if desired.

The formal definition of church growth introduced by the Academy of American Church Growth, and adopted with minor modifications by international church growth agencies, gives an insight into church growth thinking. The wording is that adopted by the British Church Growth Association:

> Church growth investigates the nature, function, structure, health and multiplication of Christian churches as they relate to the effective implementation of Christ's commission to 'Go, then, to all peoples everywhere and make them my disciples' (Matthew 28:19). Church growth seeks to combine the revealed truths of the Bible with related insights from the contemporary social and behavioural sciences. Although not linked to any one school of church growth it owes much to the formational thinking of Dr Donald McGavran.

An operational, workaday definition given by Peter Wagner is that church growth is 'all that is involved in bringing those who do not have a personal relationship with Jesus Christ into fellowship with him and into responsible church membership'.

This description of church growth bears a close resemblance to the official definition of The Salvation Army as 'a fellowship of people who have accepted Jesus Christ as their personal Saviour and Lord and whose aim is to induce others to subject themselves to the Lordship of Christ', and helps to explain why The Salvation Army has had no difficulty in identifying with the church growth movement and its thinking.

The Salvation Army exists to get people saved. 'We are a salvation people,' wrote William Booth. 'This is our speciality; getting saved, and keeping saved, and getting others saved.' Few churches have their primary aim spelt out as clearly in their name as does The Salvation Army. And not only aim, but methodology also. For the name speaks of a dynamic, vigorous body. A people mobilised and organised for action.

7

The basic concept of The Salvation Army is in fact something of a dream scenario for church growth theorists—a church continuously mobilised for the salvation of others. Church growth therefore takes the salvationist back to his roots. Its terminology may be different. But its aim and its spirit are those of the salvationist.

In view of the close identification of church growth thinking and salvationism it will not be necessary in this book to devote much space to so called church growth theology. Church growth theology emphasises that it is God's will that the lost should be sought. Every salvationist would say amen to that. But church growth theology also emphasises that it is God's will that the lost should actually be found—and that if they are not being found it might be because the search is not being conducted in the right way. That is a more startling thought for today's salvationist, though it would not have been to his forefathers, and this aspect of church growth theology with its special challenge to the contemporary Army will be dealt with further in these pages.

CHURCH GROWTH AND QUALITY GROWTH

Church growth does not stress the importance of numerical growth only, but recognises that growth must include growth in the quality of the spiritual life and commitment of the individual believer, and in the quality of the fellowship, worship and service of the Church as a whole. It calls this internal growth.

Internal growth is one of four types of growth described in church growth theology. They are here set out in Salvation Army terminology.

☐ *Internal growth.* Growth in grace of individual salvationists and in the quality and effectiveness of the total corps. Includes also the spiritual re-awakening and return to active service of soldiers who may have lapsed into nominality.

☐ *Expansion growth.* Numerical growth in the local

8

corps through new converts won, backsliders restored, transfers from other corps or churches, and transfers from the young people's corps.

☐ *Extension growth.* Numerical growth through the opening of new outposts and corps.

☐ *Bridging growth.* Numerical growth through the opening of new outposts and corps which involves the crossing of a cultural barrier, as illustrated by the Hispanic corps currently being opened in the USA.

Internal growth is by its nature infinitely more difficult to describe and measure than the other types of growth which can be measured in numerical terms. Some further light is however shed on the nature of internal growth by the following sub-divisions which draw their inspiration from the writings of Dr Orlando Costas. Internal growth of a corps is:

☐ *Growing UP*—to maturity in Christ,
☐ *Growing TOGETHER*—in Christian fellowship,
☐ *Growing OUT*—in service and outreach.
    In this classification the other types of
    growth previously mentioned are designated:
☐ *Growing MORE*—through numerical increase.

In addition to the above, any description and measurement of internal growth as relating to the individual salvationist would need to include intangible factors such as:

☐ Quality of devotional life, prayer and Scripture study, openness to the Spirit.

☐ Attendance at meetings, participation in the life and service of the corps according to ability and gift, willingness to assume responsibility, uniform wearing.

☐ Personal witnessing for Christ.

☐ Measure of sacrifice in personal giving.

☐ Distinctiveness of life-style reflecting the values of the Kingdom.

☐ Integrity in all areas of life, observance of specific Salvation Army standards.

☐ Quality of inter-personal relationships, and concern

for the welfare of fellow salvationists and those outside the corps circle.

Internal growth factors related to the corps as a whole would include:

- [ ] Percentage of soldiery fully committed and active.
- [ ] Attendance, responsiveness and sensitivity in meetings.
- [ ] Attendance at prayer and Bible study group meetings.
- [ ] Quality of fellowship and degree of openness to receiving new members.
- [ ] Availability of local leadership for activities undertaken.
- [ ] Multiple programmes of evangelistic outreach and community service and for spiritual nurture according to resources available.
- [ ] Observance of scriptural priorities in corps programme.

It will be noted that the agenda of internal growth is nothing less than the sanctification of the individual and the growth to maturity of the Body of Christ. It therefore deals with the highest ideals of Christian life, worship and service, and is a continuous process which has no end.

Church growth recognises the vital importance of this dimension of growth. It also recognises the inter-relatedness of internal growth with all other types of growth. But it also sounds a warning note. It is possible for a corps and its leadership to become too focused on this particular form of growth. Internal growth can absorb a disproportionate amount of the available resources of time, energy and money, and divert a corps from the expansion growth which ought to be its priority mission.

This book will deal mainly with expansion and extension growth (in other words with soul-winning) which are the types of growth that can be measured numerically. But consideration of internal growth will never be far removed because of the inter-action, already noted, between one type of growth and the other.

CHURCH GROWTH AND THIS BOOK

Though in one sense there is nothing new in church growth, it can nevertheless prove a complex subject. The factors that cause growth and decline are not always easy to discern, and a subject which ranges across fields as diverse as theology, biblical studies, church history, ecclesiology, missiology, evangelism, psychology, sociology, statistics, communications and group dynamics is bound to have a certain inherent complexity. To add to that complexity there is no single authoritative source to draw from. Inspiration flows from many quarters. There is also the factor that church growth has created a language of its own—a glossary issued by the Australia Southern Territory has no fewer than 216 terms—and there is the fact of overlap, whereby helpful insights partially overlap with each other creating some confusion. It is even necessary to mine deep for the more famous principles. Reading church growth can therefore be like attempting to take in a vast series of brilliant and illuminating insights but which leave one almost bewildered by the sheer richness of their diversity.

The aim of this book has therefore been, (a) to reduce the material to manageable proportions while yet providing a broad overview of the subject as a whole, (b) to write against a Salvation Army backdrop in a non-growth church situation, (c) to write for the small and medium corps in particular but not forgetting their larger brothers, (d) to attempt to nail down some of the key principles, even to the extent of naming, stating and numbering them (though not in any order of priority), (e) to propose topics for further discussion at the end of the chapters, and finally, (f) to suggest tentatively, in broad outline, a framework for action without prejudice to local initiative or territorial policy, for salvationists are activists rather than theorists.

The book has been written as a service to colleague officers, local officers and salvationists, in the hope that the information it conveys might provide the spur to thinking, discussion, further reading and then vision, planning and outworking.

Every corps has to face its own *contextual* factors—some are shared by all. These are the national trends of social life, attitudes to religion, local community factors, the district round the hall, etc. Not much, if anything, can be done about these. For example, church membership and attendance in the country as a whole are contextual factors. In the USA they are 70 per cent and 73 per cent respectively. In England they are only 11 per cent and 9 per cent. They are higher in Scotland, Wales and Northern Ireland.

Every corps is also faced with *institutional* factors. These divide into a. and b. With regard to, (a) territorial and divisional policies, ranging from people's perception of the Army, policies relating to radio and TV, our social work, matters of orders and regulations, uniform wearing, music, literature, membership requirements, etc., there is again little that the local corps can influence directly. It is when it comes to (b), those institutional factors which are under the control of the corps, that the panorama of opportunity opens up. For some these factors may not be as encouraging as they would wish. But it is one of the Army's great assets that the smallest unit has the strength and reputation and solidity of the Army as a whole behind it, whilst still having the glorious freedom to initiate, adapt and experiment.

Growth usually begins as a vision which at first is shared by a few. As the circle widens and the vision is shared by more and more the necessity for some kind of forum for sharing, for some kind of structure, for leadership, is felt. If church growth is to 'take off' there will in the end have to be a central task force under the corps officer to give it the needed impetus. This might well be the corps council, or a group formed from within it. From that group will flow the need for other task forces, working parties and groups, co-opting more and more people until everyone is caught up in the vision. Distributing copies of this book in ever widening circles and meeting to discuss the questions that are to be found at the end of the chapters, and then deciding on what action needs to be taken, might be some of the first steps towards bringing the vision of growth to fruition.

For discussion

1. To what extent does the corps accurately reflect in its life the official definition of The Salvation Army?

2. Internal growth is described as growing up, growing together, growing out. In what specific ways is internal growth in the corps being, (a) encouraged, (b) evidenced?

3. What are some of the negative, and what are some of the positive contextual factors, nationally and locally, affecting the evangelistic mission of the corps?

2
Deciding for growth

As much as anything, church growth consists of a particular *attitude* towards growth. It is an attitude in which both the leadership of the corps and the corps as a whole believe in its possibility, want it to happen, are prepared to pay the price, and are willing to make it their priority objective and to pray for it. That's deciding for growth! It leads us to consider a number of growth principles.

THE EXPECTATION PRINCIPLE

No corps can grow if it does not believe in the possibility of growth. Put in positive terms that is the Expectation Principle (number one in our list): *To grow, a corps must believe it can.* Without faith for growth there can be no growth.

The trouble with this basic principle is that for many it will seem like an insurmountable obstacle. However much they might want to believe in the possibility of growth, most of the facts around them seem to point in the opposite direction.

Painting glowing pictures from far away or long ago will do little to engender faith. The worldwide scene of Christian growth is in fact very encouraging. The Church is expanding more rapidly than at any time in its history. At a conservative estimate it is reckoned that 63,000 new Christians are added to the church every day, and that every week 1,600 new churches are opened.

But the impact of non-growth nearer at hand—the church in Britain, for example, has been declining unremittingly since the turn of the century, and in the 1970s lost one million members, 2,500 ministers and closed 1,000 churches—is stronger because it is more immediate and visible and has been directly experienced. Good news from far away and long ago can have the opposite effect to that intended. It can act as a threat with its unspoken suggestion that there must be something wrong with our own faith and commitment. An irritant because it prompts the question: 'Why there, Lord, but not here? Why then, but not now?'

Exposure to decline over a long period can have a corrosive effect on the heart and mind. Gradually and imperceptibly we adjust to lack of growth. Mental defence mechanisms spring into play to explain why there is no growth or why it is not important. These rationalisations each have a kernel of truth, but they emphasise one side of the truth only and the picture is therefore unbalanced.

Church growth thinking challenges us consciously and deliberately to face up to and reject such defence mechanisms. That is the first step towards achieving a breakthrough to renewed faith in the possibility of growth.

1. Facing up to non-growth arguments

The quality-not-quantity argument. 'We are not interested in numbers; it is the quality that counts, not the quantity,' is the line taken. The emphasis on the importance of internal growth is entirely laudable. But the flaw in the argument is that unless quality growth includes a concern for bringing others into the fellowship it will be a damaged form of quality that is produced. Groups of all kinds tend to introversion and for a corps, which exists to bring others to Christ, to neglect the quantity dimension is to lose an essential part of the quality to which it is aspiring. It is like suggesting that the shepherd should stop seeking for any more lost sheep so that the quality of life of those already in the fold might be improved.

A variant on this over-emphasis on internal growth sometimes reads: 'We are concentrating on quality growth first, and when the corps is right we will turn to expansion growth.' It may be true that a corps has to improve qualitatively to attract new people, but to separate internal and expansion growth in time is questionable. Firstly, because the church is a school for sinners there will never come a time when everything is right. The corps could be embarking on mission impossible, with expansion growth deferred for ever. Secondly, it is often an emphasis on expansion growth which lifts the corps out of itself and produces the quickest internal growth. Having to rise to new challenges and nurture new babes in Christ can do miracles for the internal growth of those involved. This is known as the outside-in theory in church growth thinking.

So in the Kingdom it is not a matter of either/or, for both quality and quantity are vital. Internal and external growth are inextricably linked.

The don't-deserve-to-grow argument. This is an expression of a deep-seated inferiority feeling which says that we are not good enough to grow. We don't deserve to. Peter Wagner calls this the 'Go to Keswick' argument, this being a reference to a missionary whose solution to all non-growth problems was to suggest that the people concerned were not spiritual enough, and that if only they would 'go to Keswick' and get spiritually re-charged there would be immediate growth. Fortunately church growth research has exploded that one. The spiritual condition of a church is of course an important factor, but is only one factor among many. It is a mistake to assume that all growing churches are more 'spiritual' than their static or declining counterparts.

The decline-is-inevitable argument. Some years ago a divisional commander found himself congratulating a

16

corps officer because the rate of numerical decline had slowed. Both laughed when they realised the irony of the situation. But in countries where the church has experienced numerical decline for half a century or more, it seems only right to offer congratulations when that decline is slowed, even if not halted or reversed. When a corps succeeds in maintaining its numerical position it is considered something of an accomplishment.

So entrenched in the mind can be the 'decline is inevitable' argument that it comes as a shock to the system to read the growth expectations which the church growth movement considers appropriate. These are for the American church scene and cannot be transferred directly to other countries where conditions are harder, but they are quoted because they offer a challenge not only to the 'decline is inevitable' but also to the 'maintaining is good' mentality:

25 per cent growth per decade	Poor
50 per cent growth per decade	Fair
100 per cent growth per decade	Good
200 per cent growth per decade	Excellent
300 per cent growth per decade	Outstanding
500 per cent growth per decade	Incredible

Though such figures are being achieved by churches in many parts of the world, even a *tenth* of such growth would still represent significant growth in some western countries. It should be mentioned that churches rarely have the physical capacity to keep doubling every 10 years, and that arrangements are usually made for daughter churches to be commenced from within the membership.

Church growth challenges our too easy acceptance of the 'decline is inevitable' argument and calls us to face up to it deliberately and ruthlessly. If there were no churches or corps growing in a particular country it would have to be accepted that until now no one has been able to discover the key to growth in that country. But if there are churches and corps that are growing it becomes a matter of priority to discover what it is that they are doing right.

The remnant argument. The remnant defence mechanism seeks to make a virtue of decline by arguing that small is beautiful. Small is holy, therefore the smaller the better. If there must be growth, then let it be slow and cautious. The all important thing is faithfulness and 'keeping the flag flying'.

This type of thinking which runs so counter to the gospel and everything the Army stands for, was nevertheless widespread in the 1960s when anything which smacked of concern for institutional survival was suspect. There is now a greater understanding that every church and denomination stands only a generation away from extinction and that it has a duty to renew itself in order to fulfil its mission.

The community service argument. The trend towards emphasising service to the community in corps life is commendable. Church growth thinking stresses the need for every church member to have opportunities to exercise their particular gifts within the Body of Christ, and many salvationists have been endowed with caring gifts. It is right that the corps should provide them with the opportunity of using them.

But even something as good as community service can provide a defence mechanism to justify a lack of numerical growth. If the aim of the corps is seen as serving the community, then any measurement of effectiveness of ministry will be in terms of the quality of that service. Numerical growth will seem an irrelevance.

Church growth thinking pleads for a balanced approach as was achieved in the Early Church. The Early Church served its members and the community in practical, caring ways, but never lost sight of the need to proclaim Christ. That remained its priority.

The sow-the-seed argument. This argument emphasises that ours is the task of sowing the seed. The reaping is something we must leave to God. What counts is the faithfulness of our sowing. Visible results are up to God.

This argument over-emphasises one side of a great truth, for the scriptural command is not only to sow but also to

18

reap. The parable of the sower (Matthew 13:3-9), for example, would end strangely if it ended with the sowing and there was no mention of harvesting. In Matthew 9:36-38 our Lord specifically asks his disciples to pray that God will send labourers into his *harvest*.

The point is even more persuasive when expressed in terms of seeking the lost. McGavran coined the term Search Theology to describe this 'theological justification of the practice of continuing to use given evangelistic methodology even though it does not result in making disciples'. Had the shepherd in our Lord's story kept on seeking the lost sheep week after week and month after month without ever finding it, questions about his efficiency would have been asked. And yet, as McGavran has pointed out, 'sometimes even empty-handedness becomes a habit and is caused by peering into ravines where there are no sheep, resolutely neglecting those who long to be found in favour of those who refuse to be. Sometimes it is a question of sticking for decades to methods which have proved ineffective.'

Church growth thinking emphasises that Jesus himself came 'to seek and to *save* that which was lost.' (Luke 19:10). Seeking alone would have been unthinkable. *'Mere search is not what God wants,'* italicises McGavran. *'God wants his lost children found.'*

The wait-for-revival argument. A retired officer confided wistfully that throughout his officership he had waited for the revival which repeatedly had been forecast as being just round the corner, but which had never come. There was a gentle unspoken reproach against God in the comment. God had let him down by not sending the revival which would have brought visible results.

Revival is God's gift. We can neither command it nor make God grant it. To tie success in evangelism to the coming of a revival is therefore to risk a lifetime of frustration, and is not how God means it to be. God is not a capricious being, sometimes giving and sometimes withholding from his servants the power they need to accomplish his work.

Church growth, in harmony with what has always been

19

the Army's teaching, stresses that the winning of the lost for the Kingdom is not dependent on revivals, however welcome and wonderful those special seasons are when God's power seems to sweep everything before it. There is never a time when God does not want his lost children found. Never a time when he is not preparing the hearts and minds of those who know him not. Never a time when his resources are not freely at the disposal of his children. The spiritual power needed to reach and win those without Christ is always available. It was not new power but new methods that changed things in 1878. The key is how to channel the power that is always there through effective methods of evangelism right for the times.

If we are to scale the barrier of the Expectation Principle, which reminds us that to grow, a corps must believe it can, it is necessary to unmask and courageously deal with these or any other rationalisations held consciously or unconsciously. They protect us against the pain of failure in numerical growth. But they sap our faith.

A second way to increase our faith in the possibility of growth is to seek to develop what is known as 'church growth eyes'.

2. Developing 'church growth eyes'

Seeing with 'church growth eyes' is more than the ability to analyse a corps situation in terms of church growth principles. It is seeing again the wonder of God's plan for the world and discerning his hand in everything around us.

Church growth eyes' and the Bible. No single step is more likely to awaken faith than to read the New Testament with 'church growth eyes'. Marking and prayerfully studying all the passages, first in Acts, then in the gospels and the epistles that deal with any aspect of church growth—from proclamation, discipline, growth, the Kingdom, gifts for service, to church planting and much more—will kindle faith as perhaps never before. Many church growth publications include Bible study guides and lists of references to aid the student.

'Church growth eyes' and the experience of others. Deliberate exposure to church growth thinking through reading books and magazines and listening to cassettes and watching videos on the subject, are ways of developing 'church growth eyes'. The ocean of negativity around us can only be counteracted by a firm determination to absorb positive 'can be done' thinking by any means open to us. The availability of such material, written against a local or similar background increases constantly, and it is now possible to share in the experiences of those who have managed to halt the deadly decline and start moving upwards. Of even greater value is to be able to see and feel and experience personally growth that is taking place in a neighbouring church or corps. Time spent with a colleague researching with 'church growth eyes' will make faith soar. It is when we think growth, talk growth, read growth, preach growth and dream growth that the barriers of unbelief come tumbling down.

'Church growth eyes' and personal experience. Not everyone has had the experience of seeing growth or being involved with it personally. But reflection on any growth experienced, however humble, and seeking to see and interpret it through 'church growth eyes' can be another great stimulation to faith. If it could happen there and then, why not here and now?

To grow, a corps must believe it can. Faith is not at our command. But there is much we can do to foster it. However, deciding for growth involves other growth principles as well.

THE LEADERSHIP COMMITMENT PRINCIPLE

No corps can grow without the officer and the local officers being committed to the idea of growth. This is the second principle in our list, the Leadership Commitment Principle: *To grow, the leadership of a corps must want it to grow and be prepared to pay the price.* The other side of the coin, that the corps as a whole must want to grow and be prepared to pay the price, will be dealt with in the next section.

Church growth is leader-orientated. In surveys of patterns of church government most conducive to growth, congregation-led churches tend to get the lowest ratings and strong-leader churches the highest. Constitutionally speaking the Salvation Army corps is set for growth. 'Growing churches always have effective leadership,' comments Roy Pointer. 'They have leaders who get the job done.'

Growth, however, carries a price tag, and like the king who went to war the leaders of a corps—corps officer and local officers—need to sit down and count the cost first.

☐ *Growth will demand time.* Time for study of church growth principles, time for discussion and sharing and arriving at a strategy. Time for working out the plans formulated. And time for the people it is hoped to reach. All of this on top of existing commitments? Not necessarily, for priorities may be seen in a different light, and delegation figures prominently on the church growth agenda. But it will undoubtedly mean much hard work.

☐ *Growth will involve the risk of failure.* Success or failure in numerical growth can be measured. Quality or service goals are more intangible, hence less risky.

☐ *Growth may mean a change of leadership style.* 'If you are a leader, exert yourself to lead,' said Paul (Romans 12:8 *NEB*). In recent years the 'enabler' model of ministry has been much in vogue, influencing also Salvation Army leadership. The picture has been that of the laity as front line soldiers in the secular world, with the pastor or officer building them up, supporting them from behind, enabling them for the ministry. There is now a reaction against this more passive form of leadership. The pastor most in demand 'is the one who provides strong leadership, makes things happen, and is somewhat of an entrepreneur'. Churches are looking for leaders, people who will lead from up-front. Peter Wagner describes the ideal church growth officer as a 'leader + equipper'—defining an equipper as 'a leader who actively sets goals for a congregation according to the will of God, obtains goal ownership from the people, and sees that each church member is properly motivated and equipped to do his or her part in accomplishing the goals'.

☐ *Growth means becoming a change agent.* 'Numerical growth means change, not more of the same,' comments Lyle E. Schaller. How to introduce change and anticipate and cope with the different responses it will evoke is now part of managerial science. Its study will be another demand on that precious time. And there cannot be change without pain!

☐ *Growth may mean people-problems.* It may mean being insistent if and when persuasion has failed. 'Trying to appease all members will hinder growth,' warns Lyle E. Schaller. 'There is a time to do what is right, regardless of cost and short term losses.' The biggest single problem facing successful churches which have seen a large influx of new people is the so-called 'Pioneer versus Homesteader' conflict, the misunderstandings between old and new.

☐ *Growth will mean a willingness to share the ministry.* Despite its emphasis on strong leadership, church growth thinking also discourages the idea of the leader doing everything. The reason why some churches of around 200—a recognised plateau in church growth— do not develop is because the minister is reluctant to share pastoral responsibility with others. Beyond 200 the talk is of the minister being a 'rancher' rather than a shepherd—that is, he has to rely on help in his shepherding of the flock. But even in the smaller church or corps, the leader who does not share the ministry can strangle growth.

☐ *Growth may mean the officer staying a long time.* Lyle E. Schaller says: 'There is overwhelmingly persuasive evidence that from a long-term congregational perspective, the most productive years of a pastorate seldom begin before the fourth or fifth or sixth year of a minister's tenure in that congregation.' That has to be balanced against the historical fact that at the time of the Army's most rapid growth, the policy was to change officers frequently, sometimes after just a few months. But the value of longer appointments in today's circumstances is increasingly being appreciated.

☐ *Growth will require dogged determination.* Every influence will be brought to bear to make the vision fade and the resolution falter. There is bound to be a long slog through the foothills before the sunnier uplands are reached. It will take determination not to turn back before then.

THE CORPS COMMITMENT PRINCIPLE

But leadership committed to growth is insufficient, for unless the corps as a whole wants growth and is prepared to pay the price—nothing will happen. Hence the third principle, the Corps Commitment Principle: *To grow, the corps as a whole must want to grow and be prepared to pay the price.* Here are some items on the price list for the corps as a whole:

☐ *Growth will mean acceptance of the growth ideal,* and a willingness to participate actively in its realisation.

☐ *Growth will mean increased demands on time and energy.* It will mean getting increasingly involved in the life of the corps, in the use of gifts and abilities.

☐ *Growth may involve assuming greater responsibility.* and opening up the leadership circle to new people.

☐ *Growth will mean willingness to accept the pain of change:* the pain of new methods, new styles, different meetings.

☐ *Growth will mean the opening up of fellowship groups* and the welcoming of new people into them.

☐ *Growth may mean moving from a single-cell to a multi-cell structure.* This can be painful for a small corps where everybody knows everyone else intimately and the corps is basically one small group.

It will be seen that growth is not a painfree prospect, either to the corps leadership or to the corps as a whole. It might be tempting to say, why bother? Some churches do in fact reach a well-reasoned conclusion that growth is not for them. They see themselves as not having a strong

24

evangelistic imperative, or deliberately decide to remain small. But for the Salvation Army corps that option does not really exist. 'A Salvation Army corps,' wrote William Booth, 'is a band of people united together to attack and Christianise an entire town or neighbourhood.' To make that harmonise with a non-growth policy would take some considerable mental gymnastics!

That getting people saved and incorporated into the life of the corps means hard work, adjustment to change, active involvement and a willingness to welcome and accept new people, is hardly news to the salvationist. The Lord's work has always called for sacrifice, and salvationists give of their time and energy as generously as any. Yet, each generation has to count the cost for itself and be prepared to bear it.

The inescapable motivating force for the salvationist is the Lord's call to seek the lost. He knows that The Salvation Army exists to get people saved and he is prepared to play his part. At its lowest, he sees it as his duty. At its highest, it is a joy for him to help the lost to be found and see them linked with the corps. He appreciates the fresh vitality that new people bring with them, their enthusiasm, their keenness to participate in everything, and in turn win others for Christ. The prospect of growth makes the true salvationist shout hallelujah! If an influx of new people brings new problems—so be it. The Early Church and the early Army knew all about that. At least they will be the problems of life, not those of death.

THE PRIORITY PRINCIPLE

The fourth principle, the Priority Principle, states: *To grow, a corps—and each group within it—must make evangelism its priority.*

Because The Salvation Army is a 'permanent mission to the unconverted' the corps as a whole, and each of its constituent parts, must give priority to evangelism. This is easily lost sight of in the day to day life in a corps. It is probably true that for many salvationists corps life consists of going to meetings and a series of practices. They would find it hard to put into a nutshell what the corps is there for.

Church growth thinking emphasises the need for a corps to have a clearly written philosophy of ministry, a statement of purpose which, in a few words, spells out the priorities and other aspects of what hopefully will be a balanced ministry. It should be an individualised statement that reflects the identity and image of that particular corps. It is not a statement for all corps everywhere.

The starting point will inevitably have to be the definitions of The Salvation Army and of a corps already noted. The glossary in *The Salvation Army Year Book* emphasises that a corps 'is a Salvation Army unit established for the propagation of the gospel'. The priority of evangelism, and the idea of 'a band of people united to Christianise an entire town or neighbourhood', will have to be the fundamental point. But the corps also has a responsibility to provide a balanced ministry on a scriptural pattern.

The following passages need to be consulted in the preparation of the statement of purpose. They contribute to our picture of the life of the Christian fellowship: Matthew 25:31-40, Matthew 28:19, Acts 1:8, Acts 2, 1 Corinthians 12:12-27, 2 Corinthians 4, Ephesians 2 and 4, Colossians 3 and 4, 1 Peter 2.

Key words might well be: evangelism, worship, fellowship, spiritual development, care, witness, service, outreach, and what happens when we come together and what happens when we go out. William Booth understood the need for a balanced ministry. 'There are two dangers that confront a corps,' he wrote. 'One danger is that in endeavouring to reach new people for Christ we neglect those already saved. The other danger is to concentrate on the needs of the converted to the extent that we neglect to reach out to those in need of Christ's saving grace.' True corps growth maintains a balance. Whilst seeing the priority of fulfilling the great commission of making disciples, it maintains a healthy body life so that folk once saved are pastured, developed, trained and utilised in God's service.

The more members of the corps able to take part in the

preliminary discussions and drawing up of drafts the more valuable the statement of purpose will be. It will then be an 'owned' document, not an imposed one. It should not be longer than around 250 words so that it can be posted permanently on the notice board and published in each edition of the corps magazine. Its statement of the corps' vision, mission and priorities will be the yardstick against which all corps activities and short term goals will eventually be measured. It will be the lodestar by which the corps will get its sense of direction.

THE PRAYER PRINCIPLE

Deciding for growth must conclude with mention of a principle so vital and obvious that not much needs to be said about it. Some principles need much explanation and very little outworking. Others need little by way of explanation, but can take a lifetime in their outworking. Praying comes in the second category. Growing churches and growing corps have always had a group of people within them engaged in constant, believing and fervent prayer for the evangelistic work being undertaken. There is no way round it. It is one of the cardinal principles of growth. Prayer awakens faith and prayer brings results. The Prayer Principle, the fifth in our list, puts it concisely: *To grow, a corps must engage continuously in believing prayer for growth.*

For discussion

1. In the light of the 'non-growth rationales' mentioned, how may faith in growth be further stimulated and the Expectation Principle reached.

2. What are some of the practical implications for the corps of the Leadership and Corps Commitment Principles?

3. What practical differences would the application of the Priority Principle make to the various aspects of corps life, and what would some of the key points be in any proposed statement of purpose?

4. How can prayer for growth be further stimulated individually and corporately?

3
Analysing for growth

Church growth has become a science, and science prides itself on its handling of facts. Church growth argues that for too long the hows and whys of growth and decline have been shrouded in a fog (a much-used church growth word). For church growth there are no questions too painful to ask, no myths too entrenched to be queried, and no taboos too sacred to challenge. It is only when we have the facts, it argues, not suppositions or opinions or wishful thinking based on tradition, that the beginnings of solutions will emerge.

This characteristic rejection of anything escapist is embodied in principle six, the Face Facts Principle, which states: *To grow, a corps needs to face the facts about itself with ruthless honesty.*

There is no church more geared up for analytical exercises based on statistics than The Salvation Army. We are inveterate pulse-takers. But now it is a matter of putting those statistics to work, of 'counting to some purpose', as Jeffrey Harris entitles his booklet on the subject.

Church growth is not an event. It is not even a campaign. It is a permanent attitude to growth and a constant but pragmatic approach to methodology. The analytic exercises suggested in this chapter should therefore not be thought of as 'one-off' events. They will need to be updated at least once a year, and may benefit from being linked with a regular yearly event like the corps anniversary or commitment Sunday.

Much of the fact gathering may have to be done by the corps officer or his immediate helpers, though a number of corps set aside task groups for this purpose. The sharing of findings, and participation in discussion leading to goal setting and action, should be as wide as possible. Talking growth leads not only to faith, but hopefully also to activity.

The exercises are of necessity set out in summarised form, and are on a 'do it yourself' basis. Increasingly, however, territories are employing independent consultants—salvationists not from that particular corps—who have been trained as church growth consultants. They are able to address the situation objectively and, after taking soundings at all levels, present a report to the corps on strengths, concerns and potential, and make their recommendations.

Analysis is only a small part of church growth. It must not be allowed to get out of proportion or 'analysis paralysis' will set in. Church growth diagnostic methods enable us to get the information needed in a methodical way. The old time corps officer had to rely more on intuition. But it was often amazing how within a matter of days he had got a grip of the situation by simply talking with key locals, visiting soldiers in need, looking at the books, listening to all and sundry, walking round the district, and generally sniffing around. The new tools at our disposal are not meant to make us into permanent analysers. Battle commanders are often ordered at a few hours' notice to take over a front bristling with complexity and have to issue the first orders within minutes. The Salvation Army lies more in that tradition than in the leisurely 'give me a year to get the feel' approach.

Having said that, however, there is no need to tackle all the diagnostic exercises in this chapter in one go. That could lead to indigestion. As long as all initiative and action is not held up while the process of diagnosis continues, there is no reason why it should not be approached in a measured way. In a small corps the

diagnosis of the statistical situation need only take a matter of hours or at the most a day or two. Follow-up discussions may, of course, take much longer.

Information for its own sake has no value. It is therefore vital for the analysis to yield results. This is achieved by asking searching questions at every 'step' of each exercise. Space will not allow for suggested questions at each stage, but the two key questions ought to be:

☐ What does this information tell us about our corps, and especially about our expansion growth?

☐ What practical steps can be taken now to begin to remedy the situation? Who will take the necessary action, and when and to whom will he report back?

There are eight exercises included in the chapter. They draw their information from the research conducted at the Fuller Institute and other similar centres. As they are set out in concentrated form it is important that every possible visual device be used in presenting the results. An imaginative approach will pay a handsome dividend. Every graph or pie-chart will be worth the proverbial thousand words.

FIRST EXERCISE—CORPS GROWTH ANALYSIS

Steps 1, 2 and 3 of this exercise measure expansion growth by its most direct indicator, growth in the number of new senior soldiers, and is therefore by far the most important of the eight exercises and their various subdivisions. The other exercises measure contributory factors which indirectly affect expansion growth. As far as numerical growth is concerned it is steps 1, 2 and 3 of the corps growth analysis exercise which are the vital barometer.

Expansion growth comes from three sources, and losses also divide into three categories. These are set out in the box which follows.

Conversion growth	Biological growth	Transfer growth
Adults who accept Jesus as personal Saviour. Includes re-enrolments following previous removals	Young people transferred from the YP corps	Transfers from other corps or churches
Loss through death	**Loss through removal**	**Loss through transfer**
Soldiers promoted to Glory	Names removed for any reason other than death or transfer	Transfers to other corps or churches

Step 1—Analysis of total soldiership growth

With the help of the *Statistics Book* draw a graph showing the total growth (or decline) in the number of senior soldiers over the last 10 years. What does it tell us?

For all its usefulness it must be recognised that the total soldiership figures is a blunt measuring instrument. The death factor can radically alter its reading, as can the degree of thoroughness and regularity with which the roll has been revised. Allowances may have to be made for such factors. But in church growth research it is not a matter of trying to look good, or of trying to kid ourselves. It is the facts that matter—whether good or bad. However, Steps 2 and 3 of this exercise enable more precise readings to be obtained.

Step 2—Analysis of growth by categories

With the help of the *Soldiers' Roll* and the *Census Minute Book* divide the soldiership gains and losses into their three respective categories for each of the 10 years. Show the details on a chart similar to the one below, distinguishing the categories by means of colours. This is a very important indicator. What does it tell us?

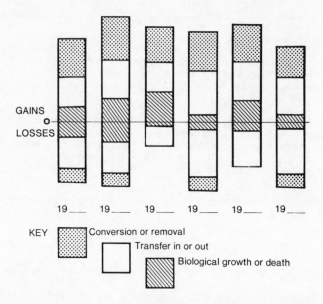

GAINS
LOSSES

19____   19____   19____   19____   19____   19____

KEY ▨ Conversion or removal
☐ Transfer in or out
▨ Biological growth or death

Note that for the purposes of researching expansion growth, growth from transfers is irrelevant. Growth through transfers may be due to the mobility of the population, the quality, size and range of activities of the losing or gaining corps, or to other factors, but however welcome such reinforcements might be they do not represent expansion growth. In measuring expansion growth only conversion and biological growth are significant. With 'church growth eyes' it can be seen that some so-called growing churches and corps are not really so. They have simply profited from a migration of sheep and need to watch lest they are lulled into false complacency.

Step 3—Analysis of conversion and biological growth by names

This is the acid test. Isolate the conversion and biological growth for each year *by names*. Set aside the names of young people who come from salvationist families. What is left are the names of those who over the last 10 years, whether as young people or adults, *have come new to the corps and have become senior soldiers*. From general knowledge, or if necessary by asking the people concerned, list how the first contact was made in each case. Was it through personal influence by someone and, if not, which of the corps programmes, meetings and activities has shown the best track record in effective evangelism?

The above research needs to be conducted in the light of some crucial facts that have emerged in church growth research. They are so important that they should be written in lights! Fourteen thousand individuals were asked why they had linked up with their church. The result, given below, has been confirmed over and over again in other polls, and may receive further confirmation through local research.

Special need	1-2 per cent
Walked in	2-3 per cent
Pastor	5-6 per cent
Visitation	1-2 per cent
Sunday-school	4-5 per cent
Evangelistic crusade	½ per cent
Church programmes and activities	2-3 per cent
Friends or relatives	75-90 per cent

The startling proportion that came through the personal influence of a friend or relative is a point that will be returned to. But the corps growth analysis has yet two further steps, this time related to attendance figures. Though not as important as the membership figures they nevertheless have a bearing on them and are indicative of the general health of the corps. The inclusion of the junior soldiers' roll figure adds another important indicator.

Step 4—Analysis of attendances and junior soldiers' roll

With the help of the *Statistics Book* add to the original diagram used in Step 1, four separate graphs showing the average weekly attendance over the 10 year period at the Sunday morning meeting, the Sunday evening meeting, the Sunday-school, and a graph showing the junior soldiers' roll. What do these indicators reveal?

Step 5—Composite growth

Church growth speaks of a composite growth figure. This is the bringing together of certain key indicators to form one composite figure. Apart from the analysis by name of new soldiers added to the roll it is probably the simplest way of charting general health and growth. Figures chosen vary. This is not important as long as there is consistency in the choice. But by way of illustration it can be mentioned that the corps in the Australian territories now work on the following formula:

Soldiers' roll (multiplied by two)
Junior soldiers' roll
Adherents' roll
Home league average weekly attendance
Main Sunday meeting average weekly attendance.

These five figures added together and then divided by five give the composite strength figure. The unusual multiplication by two of the soldier figure is in order to 'weight' the key factor in the formula. However arrived at, a composite figure enables an easily grasped decadal chart line to be drawn to indicate the general numerical position.

What kind of a picture does the composite strength graph for the last 10 years give?

Before moving on to the second exercise we need to note two terms frequently used in church growth research. The *Annual Growth Rate* (AGR) which refers to soldiership growth using data from two consecutive years, and the *Decadal Growth Rate* (DGR) which refers to soldiership growth over a 10 year period. The terms are sometimes used also in reference to the composite growth.

SECOND EXERCISE—CORPS WORKERS AND ACTIVITIES ANALYSIS

This exercise has to do with the leaders and active workers in the corps and the activities they engage in.

Church growth distinguishes five types of leaders/workers within church life:

☐ *Class one leaders/workers.* These are the maintenance leaders/workers who are concerned especially with the internal growth of the corps. They hold senior and YP local officer commissions, are company guards, songsters, bandsmen, welcome sergeants, leaders of Bible study groups etc.

☐ *Class two leaders/workers.* These are the outreach leaders/workers who are concerned especially with outreach to those in the community who need Christ. Their numbers include pub boomers, open-air meeting workers, visitors of non-Army families, leaders of outreach-orientated house groups, league of mercy members, etc.

☐ *Class three leaders.* These are envoys or other employees who are unpaid or partially paid.

☐ *Class four leaders.* The corps officers and other full-time paid staff of the corps.

☐ *Class five leaders.* Divisional, territorial and international leaders.

It is the class one and two leaders/workers that will concern us in this exercise. They represent the active work-force of the corps. Attenders at meetings but who otherwise do not take an active part in the corps are listed as 'attenders only'.

Achieving the right balance between maintenance and outreach workers is so important for expansion growth that it becomes principle seven, the Balanced Work-force Principle. *To grow, a corps needs to achieve the right balance between maintenance and outreach leaders/workers.*

Step 1—Analysis of corps activities

Under the two headings of 'Maintenance' and 'Outreach', list all the activities that take place in the corps. The list should include meetings, sectional activities, practices, fellowships, house groups, YP meetings and clubs and parades, coffee mornings, charity shop—everything.

In attempting this exercise it will immediately become evident that some activities seem to fall in both categories. For example, the home league may be thought of as mainly maintenance, and yet may turn out to be the chief source of new soldiers. Or the band may be thought of as internal, and yet open air work is obviously outreach. No clear rules can be given. It will depend on the *main* emphasis of each particular section in each particular corps.

These lists will reveal, firstly, the total range of activities in the corps, and secondly, whether they are chiefly directed toward maintenance or outreach. Turning the information into percentages will further clarify the picture: x per cent of activities devoted to maintenance, x per cent to outreach. What does this information tell us? Is there an imbalance between the two columns?

Step 2—Analysis of types of workers and time spent

This analysis divides into two parts. In part 1, list in a column all *types* of maintenance leaders/workers that are at work in the corps—company guards, senior and YP local officers, songsters, welcome sergeants, etc.

In a second column add the number of such workers there are in the corps, for example, company guards: 10. In a third column estimate the hours each worker devotes to preparing or doing his work, eg, company guards: three hours weekly for preparation, visitation and presentation. Allow a fourth column for totals. The following box gives a partial view of how the form will look.

In part 2, do a similar exercise by listing all the types of outreach workers there are in the corps, those whose main or specific task is to seek to reach and minister to those outside the corps. Again some very fine judgments will have to be made as to what constitutes maintenance as over against outreach, and where dual or even plural commissions are held it may be necessary to count those

Maintenance workers	Total number in corps	Average hours per week	Total hours per week
1. Company guards	10	3	30
2. Bandsmen	12	6	72
3. etc.			

individuals in each category. As with part 1, list the number of workers in each category and estimate the individual and total hours spent.

Bring parts 1 and 2 together. Compare the number of maintenance workers with the number of outreach workers. Compare the number of hours spent each week on maintenance and outreach activities. What do these comparisons say about the corps? Compare your findings

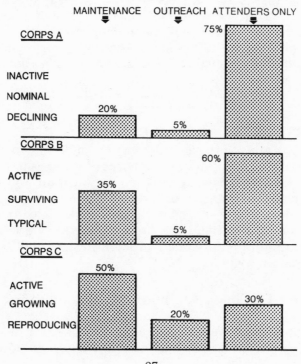

with the diagram on page 37. If your corps is in the 'A' or 'B' category, what practical steps can be taken to rectify the imbalance in leaders/workers and activities undertaken?

THIRD EXERCISE—SYMPTOMS OF SICKNESS ANALYSIS

This and the next exercise deal with the more intangible factors of quality, the kind of factors that cannot be found in any book of statistics. One of the more frequent analogies used of the Church in the New Testament is 'the Body of Christ'. From this biological analogy concepts of growth and development flow naturally. So do also medical concepts such as health and sickness, vital signs and symptoms of disease. From the publication of Peter Wagner's *Your Church can be Healthy* has flowed a literature of church pathology!

The symptoms of sickness analysis is a way of giving your corps a qualitative check-up. Ten common illnesses that can befall corps will be named and their chief symptoms described. It is suggested that a corps should rate itself under each disease in one of the following four categories:

A very serious problem	A major problem	A minor problem	No problem

Rating in any but the last category should lead to urgent consideration, corps disease by corps disease, as to what practical steps can be taken in the short, medium and long term, to ensure that health returns. Wallowing in symptoms will do no one any good! Rating can be done in small groups, or initially singly and then compared and discussed in small groups, before being brought to the attention of the corps as a whole.

Step 1—Check for maintenance complex

Maintenance complex is an almost exclusive preoccupation by a corps and its leadership with its own life and affairs. Symptoms include an imbalance between maintenance and outreach workers, a preponderance of activities designed for the corps membership itself, most of the time, energy and resources of the corps leadership devoted to internal growth, with corps council meeting agenda being dominated by the recurring cycle of corps and sectional events, property and finance matters, and all the other concerns of an inwards-turned group. If this is a problem, one remedy is to seek to achieve a higher proportion of workers and activities that are outreach oriented. What other solutions suggest themselves?

Step 2—Check for failure syndrome

Failure syndrome is a close brother to the 'decline-is-inevitable' argument already discussed. Its symptoms are a negative attitude to growth generally and a 'we've tried it all before and it doesn't work' attitude to any specific proposals for outreach. Its leaders seem to have a built-in 'no'. The corps gives a tired and dispirited impression. If this is a problem, a deliberate and concerted attempt to recover faith in the possibility of growth, as set out in chapter 2 of this book, is one remedy. What other steps can be taken to deal with the problem?

Step 3—Check for ethnikitis

Ethnikitis describes the situation when people of a different ethnic background and language move into the immediate area around the corps. What is the corps to do? Adopt a 'mission' philosophy ministry, and abandon building a traditional corps structure? Seek to move, as to remain seems to invite a lingering death! Have two congregations within the same building? Relate by way of the children who speak English? It is a real problem to many corps, particularly in the inner cities. Are there other solutions that fit the local setting?

Step 4—Check for age imbalance

Age imbalance or 'old age' or 'ghost town disease' as

it is sometimes called, refers to the situation where 'funerals significantly outnumber weddings' in the corps. Diagrams showing by means of blocks the percentage of members within each 5-year age segment can be prepared. They will confirm statistically and visually whether it is a 'young age' or 'old age' corps. But such information can also be gained by simply looking round! If it is a problem, and there are young people in the area, it may be necessary to give increased attention to the corps programmes that cater for the younger age groups. If the corps lies in an area from which young people are moving away, or in a retirement area, the solution may be for the corps to make it its declared policy to cater imaginatively for older people, without attempting to cover the full gamut of age groups. What other steps might be taken?

Step 5—Check for fellowshipitis

Fellowshipitis, also known as 'koinonitis' or 'closed shop' or 'fellowship saturation', refers to the disease of over-active fellowshipping in the corps as a whole or in any of its constituent groups. It is too much of a good thing. Fellowshipitis describes a people turned in on themselves, a closed shop, a holy huddle, us four and no more! It is groups that refuse to divide when they have become too large. It is emphasis on internal growth gone wrong. If this is a problem, one remedy is to seek to inspire all existing groups within the corps to become more open; another is to begin new groups, or to emphasise community caring. What other remedies suggest themselves?

Step 6—Check for people blindness

People blindness or inflexibility, is when a corps fails to reach out to people around them in terms that they can understand and accept. There is no attempt to reach across cultural or social barriers. The unstated message conveyed is 'be like us and you will be welcome'. This problem can be especially acute where there has been a change of population in the area and the corps has failed to adjust. Where the difficulty exists it may be necessary to take determined action to serve the needs of the people around the corps and to seek to ensure that they feel at ease when they come to any event.

Step 7—Check for complacency

This disease, also known as 'St John's syndrome' from the reference in Revelation 2:4 to the church that lost its first love, is sadly characteristic of second generation corps. As has been commented, 'the further we get from the Army's beginnings, the more liable we are to forget that we are a *Salvation* Army'. If it is a problem, one possible solution is an increased emphasis on spiritual renewal, another is to work for a steady influx of new converts. What other steps can be taken to re-awaken a complacent corps to its divine mission?

Step 8—Check for overcrowding

Overcrowding, or sociological strangulation, is likely to affect the larger corps rather than the smaller. It is satisfying to see the hall full on a Sunday morning, but that according to church growth thinking is the danger point. It invites complacency. When facilities reach 80 per cent capacity it is time to watch out and start planning for further growth. Dreaming of a new hall may not be the best or a realisable solution. Two meetings on Sunday morning, or 'parenting' an outpost or another corps, are cheaper and more effective alternatives. The world's largest church, the Yoido Full Gospel Church in Seoul, Korea, holds seven consecutive services every Sunday, starting at 6 am with attendances of 50,000 at each.

Step 9—Check for structural strain

Structural strain is when the organisational structure of the corps is not keeping abreast with developments or potential. Its most common symptom is a lack of local officers and workers to staff present and potential activities. But symptoms can also take a subtler form. For example, the Army's strong central leadership system allows for decisiveness and forceful action leading to growth, but unless there is increasing delegation as growth occurs there is a danger that the emphasis on central leadership will limit any expansion to what can personally be coped with. The accelerator can become the brake. If there are signs of structural strain, what are some of the avenues that could be explored to ease it?

Step 10—Check for factional tension

Another disease which may be present in a corps is factional tension. This refers to personal tension or animosity between leaders or between factions in the corps. Sadly the symptoms are too well known to need description. The disease is as old as New Testament times but where it breaks out it always hinders growth. Newcomers sense the tensions and do not wish to be part of such a scene and withdraw. Where this problem exists there may need to be a healing of relationships before growth can occur. What practical steps might be taken to initiate such healing?

This completes the pathology evaluation. For most corps there is much to consider, discuss and to take action on. But still continuing on the medical model, it is possible to look for positive signs of health in that part of the Body of Christ which is the corps. Where there is health there will be growth. As with the pathology evaluation there is an indebtedness to Dr Peter Wagner, and also to the adaptations made by Dr Eddie Gibbs and Dr Roy Pointer, for the church growth evaluation of vital signs of health which follows.

FOURTH EXERCISE—SIGNS OF HEALTH ANALYSIS

The following 10 features which are characteristic of growing corps, may, as with the pathology evaluation, be considered individually first, then discussed in groups before being brought before the corps as a whole. It is suggested that the following ratings for these signs of health be used:

Very strong	Strong	Weak	Very weak

Again, rating in the last two categories should lead to consideration by the corps, sign by sign, as to what practical steps might be taken to get fit again.

Most of these signs of health appear also as growth principles in this book.

Step 1—Check for effective leadership

It has already been noted that growing corps have effective leaders, from the corps officer, through the ranks of the local officers, to everyone who bears some responsibility. How clear is this vital sign in the corps? How can the situation be improved? Is there need to spot and encourage new talent, need for one generation to hand over to the next?

Step 2—Check for unity of purpose

This sign of health is also known as 'agreed agenda'. Is the chariot being pulled in the same direction by everyone? Or is it at a standstill because people are trying to pull it in different directions? Do all the sections and the corps as a whole know, agree with and fully support the corps' purposes and priorities, even when it is to their cost? If this vital sign is not too clear, a way of strengthening it may be to consider preparing a formal statement of purpose as outlined in chapter 2 of this book.

Step 3—Check for believing and constant prayer

Dr Eddie Gibbs has reminded us that prayer was at the heart of the Early Church. They prayed for guidance (Acts 1:24), for boldness (Acts 4:23-33), that others might receive the Spirit (Acts 8:15-17), to raise the dead (Acts 9:32-41), that prisoners would be freed (Acts 12:5), for missionaries (Acts 13:1-3) and for the welfare of the Church and its leaders. 'I do not know of any growing church which is not a praying church,' he adds, 'but I do know lots of praying churches which are not growing churches.' Prayer must be believing, consistent prayer of the mountain-moving kind. How evident is that vital sign and is there something additional that should be done?

Step 4—Check for life-related Bible teaching

It is the churches which give the Bible its rightful authority, teach it clearly, and demand commitment and discipline from its membership which are the growing ones. There is a cry from the heart wanting to know what the Bible has to say to today's situation. What is the state of that vital sign in our corps? Should there be further emphasis on Bible teaching and study, should there be greater emphasis on the disciplined living it enjoins? If so, what practical steps can be taken by the corps as a whole?

Step 5—Check for inspiring and eventful worship

The Sunday meetings are the 'shop window' of the corps, the focal point toward which everything else tends. Will they attract and hold and make new people want to return? Is there a sense of anticipation about them, are they inspiring, is there plentiful participation by others, does the Bible message come over strongly and clearly, is there a challenge to everyone and a feeling of responsiveness, is everyone behind those taking part, supporting them in prayer and faith? Does this vital sign need attention?

Step 6—Check for growth groupings

Apart from the single-unit small corps, corps consist of a variety of groupings, groupings which come together for the Sunday meetings. More will be said about such groupings in chapter 6, but it is important that as many cells or 'fellowship groups' as possible should be in existence, that they should not be closed but open fellowships, and that everyone who wishes to belong to such a group has this opportunity. Now that halls are no longer open every night of the week for a public meeting it is the groups that must replace the function performed by those meetings. New people cannot be held if nothing happens from one Sunday to the next. How strong is this vital sign in the corps? Is there anything that needs doing?

Step 7—Check for mobilised membership

Is the corps like the local football stadium on a Saturday afternoon where one per cent of those present do all the running about while 99 per cent just sit there, occasionally encouraging but as often criticising? The corps worker analysis will have given a fairly clear picture of the situation. A growing corps is one in which every able-bodied soldier is playing his part within the limitations of his or her circumstances. How strong is this vital sign? What can be done to encourage any remaining 'attenders only' to be active participants?

Step 8—Check for continuous evangelism

Evangelism is not only the occasional special campaign, nor is it only the regular evangelistic events like open-air meetings, pub booming, visitation or the salvation meeting. Evangelism takes place when the corps as a whole sees everything it does as a conscious and ongoing outreach to those without Christ. Evangelism is when each individual soldier sees himself using his particular gifts directly or indirectly to reach others with the good news. More will be said about continuous evangelism in later chapters. But what is the reading of this vital sign? How can the evangelistic outreach of the corps be strengthened?

Step 9—Check for compassionate service

The Salvation Army links evangelism and community service because Christ did. If our Saviour-Lord saw that salvation had to be more than soul salvation, it had to be whole salvation, who are we to attempt to draw a distinction between them? As General Frederick Coutts has aptly quoted in this connection: 'What God hath joined together let no man put asunder.' How is this vital sign? Is the corps community-conscious? What needs around it does it specifically seek to meet? How is the money in the community fund spent? Are there specific steps that need to be taken?

Step 10—Check for new-member incorporation

When new people come, how geared is the corps to welcome them, to assimilate them and incorporate them into the fellowship? The vital step is the one after the warm handshake at the door. Unless there is an immediate opening up of a group that will genuinely welcome the newcomer as a friend, the warm handshake at the door can be the handshake of farewell. How good is the corps at bringing newcomers into the inner fellowship of the corps and encouraging them into active service—if appropriate—at once? This vital sign may not have had much practical testing in some corps, but is there anything that needs to be done to ensure all will be well when needed?

There is much in both the symptoms of illness analysis and the signs of health analysis to occupy the thinking of individual salvationists, small groups, sections, the corps council and the corps as a whole for many months, and these exercises also provide the material for an 'annual check up'. But there are other exercises which can be added. They will not take so much space to describe though doing them may prove as demanding—and enlightening.

FIFTH EXERCISE—STRENGTHS AND CONCERNS ANALYSIS

This exercise, which can replace the sickness and health orientated ones or be additional to them, is important because of its positive emphasis on the strengths which a corps is perceived to have.

Every corps has strengths. Some of these strengths will be derived from belonging to The Salvation Army as a whole. The local corps benefits from the Army's good name, high visibility, and so on. These are real strengths. But each local unit will also have particular strengths. It is essential that these be recognised, for a fundamental principle of growth is the Work from Strengths Principle: *To grow, a corps needs to recognise and work from its strengths.* This is principle number eight in our list.

One corps, for example, may be particularly strong in the area of community service. The salvationists may have special caring and practical gifts, and the building facilities may offer opportunities for meals to be served and for fellowship to be offered in comfortable surroundings. This is their outstanding strength. That corps must recognise and work from its strength if it is to grow. For that corps to try to become band orientated would be sheer madness. But equally, a corps with a 36-strong band at its centre, must also work from its strengths. Many growing churches have made music their speciality and each service is a musical feast which draws by its very quality. New members are quickly assimilated into a variety of musical expressions according to individual ability and interest. Music becomes the vehicle of both evangelism and assimilation into the fellowship. We do not destroy our strengths, we work from them, and to grow, a corps needs to identify and work from the strengths it already has.

When listing strengths, past successes in outreach and new member incorporation should also be included.

The exercise can be done in a variety of ways. Selected salvationists, or all members of the corps, can be given slips of paper asking them to list 10 'strengths' which they feel the corps has, and 10 'concerns' which they have for the corps. After collation and analysis, these findings can become the basis for discussions in a number of forums—ranging from the corps council to sectional devotionals to gatherings after the Sunday night meeting or other weeknight occasions. The emphasis should be on *appreciating* and thanking God for our strengths and seeing how they can best be used. With regard to the concerns the emphasis should be on fixing the problem rather than on fixing the blame.

Another way of employing this exercise is to use it as a basis for a corps seminar. Hand out the slips of paper there and then and ask those present to complete them. Then divide into small groups for preliminary comparison, analysis and discussion. Finally bring findings together using a display board to write 'strengths' and 'concerns' in order of felt priority. As always this would lead to consideration of what practical action steps might be taken with regard to each item.

SIXTH EXERCISE—FIRST IMPRESSIONS ANALYSIS

In seeking to become expansion growth orientated, salvationists have found it helpful to imagine themselves coming to a Sunday meeting for the first time and noting everything as seen through the eyes of a newcomer. Many problems have been rectified at once as a result, and everyone has become more newcomer conscious. Participants should be asked to complete a questionnaire similar to the one below, and the exercise should conclude on the note of 'action to be taken'.

Imagine that you have walked into the corps building as a complete stranger one Sunday in order to attend a meeting:

☐ What are your first impressions of the corps building, parking facilities and immediate environment?

☐ What happens when you first enter the building?

☐ What are your impressions based on the people you first meet?

☐ Do you feel comfortable as you first come in?

☐ Are you ignored or avoided by most of the people there?

☐ Do you feel that you are really welcome there or do they simply display a formal politeness?

☐ What are your impressions of the meeting? Does it speak your language and speak to your need?

☐ Does there seem to be a spiritual excitement or dynamic within the meeting and among the people? Or is the meeting contrived and little more than a series of rituals?

☐ When the meeting is over, what happens?

☐ Is it easy to feel that you can become part of their corps, or would it take considerable effort?

☐ After you have left, do you have any desire or reason or need to go back again?

☐ During the week that follows, is there interest shown in you by anyone?

SEVENTH EXERCISE—CORPS COMMUNITY ANALYSIS

An individual or a small group can be asked to prepare a formal analysis of the corps district. It will help to define the scope of the community, to discern significant and distinct groups of people, and help the corps to discover particular opportunities for its work and witness. Much of this information will be generally known and it is not suggested that a thorough-going sociological analysis be attempted.

Each type of church has its own characteristic challenges and opportunities, and the analysis should help to define whether the corps is inner city, mid-town, suburban, newtown, housing estate, village or other. Church growth literature offers practical proposals for outreach in various categories.

It is also suggested that on a map of the area, with the

corps as its centre, three concentric circles should be drawn, of one mile, two miles and three miles respectively, and that a thorough analysis be made of the population living reasonably close to the hall, and their needs. What is the nature of the population? Does it differ from one area to another? Which areas are likely to be most receptive? Are there special needs that have not yet been recognised? What means would be most effective for each particular area? Could outposts be opened? Are there salvationists living in the proposed areas who would be willing to allow their homes to be used as bases? Would other salvationists be prepared to assist at the new opening, or even transfer there?

Such considerations of strategy starting from the community rather than the corps itself can often be most enlightening, helpful and challenging.

EIGHTH EXERCISE—CORPS BUDGET AND CORPS COUNCIL MINUTES ANALYSIS

The exercise divides into two parts and is a simple way of further testing how maintenance orientated or outreach orientated a corps is.

Ask the corps treasurer to analyse the yearly budget of the actual annual expenditure with a view to dividing it into the percentage spent on maintenance and the percentage spent on outreach. The exercise will require some complex value judgments. For example, expenditure on the hall and for heat and light will have to be proportioned out according to the approximate use of the hall for maintenance and outreach activities. Similarly, the corps officer's allowance will have to be divided according to his own estimate of the time he devotes to maintenance and outreach each week. By the nature of things, the total percentage of expenditure devoted to maintenance is likely to exceed that spent on outreach. But if the proportion spent on evangelism is only a very small percentage of the total, consideration may need to be given to re-allocating resources which can be specifically devoted to evangelism. Growth will require a financial investment.

The part of the exercise devoted to the corps council consists simply of checking the minutes of the last 10 meetings in order to ascertain what percentage was devoted to maintenance items and what percentage to considerations of outreach. The result can prove encouraging or challenging. Corrective steps, if needed, suggest themselves.

In conclusion

As mentioned earlier, there is no need for all these exercises to be attempted at once. They can be used as 'check lists' over a long period, as long as all action is not deferred until they have all been completed! Some of the exercises may not be applicable and can simply be omitted. The purpose of them is to give a full and complete picture of the corps as seen from a number of angles. These impressions will crystallise into a series of facts. It is what is done with the facts that is all important. Looking the other way is one option. Facing them, but doing nothing is another. Facing them and taking the first steps towards appropriate action is the ideal.

For discussion

1. What does the corps growth analysis reveal about the corps, and what action steps suggest themselves?

2. What does the corps workers and activities analysis reveal about the corps, and what action steps suggest themselves?

3. What does the check on 10 symptoms in the symptoms of sickness analysis reveal about the corps, and what action steps suggest themselves in any areas needing attention?

4. What does the check on 10 signs in the signs of health analysis reveal about the corps, and what action steps suggest themselves in any areas needing attention?

5. What does the strengths and concerns analysis reveal about the corps, and what are the reasons for thanksgiving and the causes for concern?

6. What does the first impressions analysis reveal about the corps, and what action steps might suggest themselves?

7. What does the corps community analysis reveal and what practical action steps suggest themselves in the light of its findings?

8. What does the corps budget and corps council minutes analysis reveal, and what action steps might suggest themselves?

4
Planning for growth

Correct analysis of the corps situation is important. And the 'check up' cannot be made once and for all. The vital signs have to be monitored regularly and a watch kept for any symptoms of disease. But however important diagnosis might be, it is only the preliminary part of a continuing process. Unless it is followed by a prescription for remedying anything that has been found to be wrong it will have been a waste of time.

To grow, a corps needs to have a definite strategy for growth. That is the ninth principle, the Growth Strategy Principle. A corps must know its evangelistic goals and have measurable plans that are realistic and appropriate for achieving those goals.

But evangelism is a many-sided subject, and before we can arrive at a strategy we need to consider it from a number of angles. Each insight has something to contribute to our understanding of it.

WAYS OF LOOKING AT EVANGELISM

1. Crusade, Saturation and Body Evangelism

In the last 25 years evangelistic strategy within the churches as a whole has gone through three distinct

53

phases. Crusade evangelism, identified with a big name like Billy Graham, appeared in the 50s. Saturation evangelism, whereby attempts are made to reach everyone living within a certain area through the mobilising of every available Christian, was emphasised in the 60s. Body evangelism, which can be defined as 'a perspective which emphasises the goal of evangelism as making disciples who are incorporated into the Body of Christ, the result of which is church growth', is the aspect which church growth thinking has emphasised from the 70s onwards. Each type has its own contribution to make and each complements the others.

2. Types 0, 1, 2 and 3 Evangelism

By dividing evangelism into types identified by a number, church growth thinking has provided a useful shorthand framework for considering the subject from four angles. The numbers refer to cultural barriers that have to be crossed. E-0 is evangelism aimed at bringing nominal church members to a commitment to Christ. There are no cultural barriers to be crossed for nominal members are familiar with the facts of the gospel. It is sad but true, as William Temple has commented, that the Church is not only a *force* for, but also a *field* for evangelism.

E-1 refers to near-neighbour evangelism, the reaching out to non-Christians of a similar culture. The barriers that exist are the differences in outlook and understanding between committed Christians and unbelievers. This is sometimes referred to as the 'stained glass' barrier. Most evangelism conducted by corps in western countries is of the E-1 type and every salvationist will be familiar from personal experience with the barriers referred to. The barriers may be formidable, but do not include the crossing of cultural barriers of language and customs.

E-2 refers to evangelism across a relatively small ethnic, cultural, or linguistic barrier—such as when La Maréchale opened the Army's work in France. E-3 is evangelism across a much larger ethnic, cultural or linguistic barrier—

such as when Commissioner Booth-Tucker began the Army's work in India. Such 'bridging growth' was formerly always associated with missionary work in other countries, but with the increase in multi-ethnic societies, E-2 and E-3 evangelism is now a frequent pattern in the western world. Church growth thinking recognises that the 'melting-pot' theory, the point of view that people of differing cultural backgrounds will automatically develop a commonness and oneness because they are in geographic proximity, is likely to be a slow process. It is increasingly acknowledged that for evangelistic strategy to be effective the 'stew-pot theory', the recognition that cultural groups may wish to keep a certain cultural identity, has to be taken into account in such situations.

3. Presence, Proclamation and Persuasion Evangelism

Another way of looking at evangelism is to consider it as Presence, Proclamation or Persuasion. Church growth thinking describes these types of evangelism as follows:

Presence Evangelism is the witness of works, the witness of 'good deeds or miraculous events which provide a starting point for explaining the gospel'. The Salvation Army's high profile as a caring movement and our use of the uniform contribute to making the Army very effective at presence evangelism. This effectiveness is enhanced if the Army's well-deserved reputation for social work generally is complemented by community service locally. In the Army's early days it was a definite evangelistic strategy to seek out 'the worst person in the place'. The miraculous transformation of such a person was presence evangelism at its most powerful, often leading to a whole chain of conversions.

Proclamation Evangelism is the witness of words, the presenting of the good news of Jesus Christ in such a way that people can hear and respond. In corps life this takes many forms. Much of the programme of the YP corps would come in this category, as would open-air meeting work, the selling of *The War Cry,* sectional activities such as the home league, over-60s club, youth club, the Sunday meetings, and any other aspects of the corps programme in which there is opportunity for the gospel to be proclaimed by word. Proclamation is an essential part of evangelism. But what church growth emphasises is that to leave the evangelistic process at the proclamation stage is to leave out the most vital part of the process, namely that of persuasion.

Persuasion Evangelism is that evangelism which has as its stated goal the conversion of non-Christians and their incorporation into the Body of Christ'. Here again church growth thinking takes the Army back to its roots. No point was more forcibly made by William Booth to his followers than that mere proclamation of the gospel was insufficient. His headings under the title 'How to Bring Sinners to God' in *Orders and Regulations for Field Officers,* first published in 1886, remain a continual reminder of persuasion evangelism at its best:

- ☐ Go to them
- ☐ Attract them
- ☐ Interest them
- ☐ Convict them
- ☐ Remove their hindrances
- ☐ Urge them to decide
- ☐ Bring them to repentance
- ☐ Lead them into faith
- ☐ Give them after-care

'The salvationist's aim in caring for a convert,' he writes under the last point, 'should be to establish him in the things of God: also to make him a fighter for God and souls.' True incorporation into the Body of Christ.

Persuasion evangelism is the most demanding of the three types of evangelism, and this is perhaps a reason why the Army—in company with most churches—is better at Presence and Proclamation than at Persuasion.

A number of outreach activities which at one time had a marked Persuasion content have tended to lapse into being solely Proclamation. Even the mercy seat appeal can become perfunctory, and 'fishing'—personal dealing—in prayer meetings has largely disappeared. Seeing a copy of the one time popular illustration of salvationists in a lifeboat reaching out to rescue sinners in the sea, a child innocently asked: 'Why are they shaking hands with the people in the sea?' Has a rescue operation subtly turned into a hand-shaking one?

In *Balanced Church Growth,* Ebbie C. Smith, has extended Presence, Proclamation and Persuasion to include *Perfecting* and *Participation* as part of the full evangelistic cycle. This adds another helpful way of looking at the subject.

4. 'Come' and 'Go' Evangelism

A further useful insight is provided by dividing evangelism into 'come' and 'go' strategies. A 'come' strategy describes the whole range of meetings, events and activities, whether at the hall, public buildings or homes, to which people might be invited to come. Some of these events and activities will be overtly evangelistic. Others, such as a coffee morning, a keep-fit fellowship, a youth club or a drama night, may be less so. But a comprehensive 'come' strategy provides a range of possibilities, and sees evangelistic potential in every 'come' activity.

'Go' evangelism, on the other hand, describes the activities that send God's people out into the streets, into homes, into factories and schools, and wherever people can be contacted. In order to grow it is important that a corps should have a balanced programme of come-structures and go-structures and that they be used to full advantage.

5. Other ways of looking at evangelism

But there are still other ways of looking at the many-sided subject of evangelism. Some of the headings from the admirable *A Guide to Evangelism* (Edited by Clive Calver, Derek Copley, Bob Moffett and Jim Smith, published by Marshalls), will serve as a reminder of the range of possibilities open, and warn us against the danger of falling into and staying in set ruts when it comes to evangelistic methodology.

Reaching People: bearing in mind their age.
Children, youth, young couples, parents of small children, childless couples, the retired, single people.
Reaching People: bearing in mind where they live.
Inner city, flat dwellers, corporation estates, owner occupiers, bedsits and sheltered housing, halls of residence, nurses' homes, satellite communities.
Reaching People: bearing in mind what they do.
Landowners, industry, itinerants, professionals and self-employed, service personnel, office shop workers, the hospitalised.

A selection of further headings from the same handbook will point to still further evangelistic possibilities. Evangelism through music, drama, literature, films, radio and TV, home meetings, parent-teacher associations, video meetings, meetings in pubs, the local media, school gate, coffee bars, supper and luncheon clubs, men's breakfasts, schools, street happenings, visitation, evangelistic surveys, small groups, holiday clubs, celebration events, and outreach to ethnic minoritites.

These various ways of looking at evangelism broaden our perspective. It is from the richness of the insights that a coherent, workable strategy which is within our resources has to be planned. But there are three further key growth principles relating to strategy that need to be considered.

THREE BASIC GROWTH PRINCIPLES RELATING TO EVANGELISM

1. The Soldier-Disciple Principle

The first of these principles, number 10 in our list thus far, is the Soldier-Disciple Principle. *To grow, a corps must have as its evangelistic aim the making of soldier-disciples.* The disciple principle is one of the foundation stones of church growth thinking. Jesus did not say, 'Go and get decisions.' He said, 'Go and make disciples'. Too much evangelism has concentrated on bringing the unbeliever to a point of decision only, and there has been inadequate interest in and arrangements for proper follow-up. As a result many babes in Christ have died at birth or soon after. Church growth thinking reinforces what has always been the basic Army position, that the evangelistic task is not complete until the convert has been incorporated into the Body of Christ and has become a responsible, active, member who, in turn, generates growth.

In Salvation Army terminology that means the evangelistic task is not complete until the convert has become a senior soldier. Had Jesus spoken in Army terms he would have said, 'Go and make soldiers.' Obviously salvationists would not in any way seek to discourage someone who decides for Christ and already has links with a particular church from returning to that church and becoming incorporated there. It is taken as a matter of course that sheep that belong elsewhere should be helped to make their way back to their own folds. But in practice such instances are rare. The evangelistic mission touches mostly those who have no strong connections with a church, and by the time the point of decision is reached so many links will have been formed with the local corps that the person is unlikely to want or need to seek another fellowship. So it is right, it is scriptural, it is the Lord's own command: a corps must have as its evangelistic aim the making of soldier disciples.

This very basic and yet simple insight can have profound consequences. Suddenly the evangelistic task becomes focused to a far greater degree than before. It is not only a matter of sowing seed, or seeking lost sheep, or of having seekers. It is a matter of reaping, of finding, of bringing to a decision, and then of nurturing and training, and of actual incorporation into the body as members. Only at that point can the evangelistic task be said to be completed. And even then Perfecting and Participation will still be in their early stages. We rejoice when there are seekers at the mercy seat, but the time of greatest rejoicing should be when new soldiers are enrolled, for this is when the process of evangelism reaches its culmination. The number of such enrolments in a year also provides the best barometer reading regarding the effectiveness of the evangelistic strategy of the corps.

How should junior soldiership be viewed in this context? With its historic concept of a junior corps with junior soldiers, The Salvation Army has a more developed philosophy of junior membership than most denominations. Is the enrolment of a junior soldier into the junior corps to be considered the equivalent of the enrolment of a senior soldier? Or is it to be seen more as a preliminary phase leading to full adult membership later? Both theological and practical points are touched upon in these questions.

There can be no minimum age for entry into the Kingdom of God. A child can know Christ at a very tender age. Any eventual incorporation into the outward and visible Body of Christ, which in the Army pattern is possible from the age of seven onwards, must be considered a most significant development. Historically the YP corps has been seen as a junior version of the senior corps, with the junior soldiers being active and responsible members of the corps and even youthful evangelists in their own right. In practice, however, it has proved difficult to attain that ideal. Perhaps it is not to be wondered at when one considers that children are still in a formative stage. To expect them to understand all the implications of Christian discipleship is asking a great deal. So, parallel with the high concept of junior soldiership, the Army has also insisted—in harmony with churches generally—that it is at the point of entry into adulthood that full membership of the Body of Christ must be consciously affirmed.

Junior soldiership can therefore be said to be more than just a preliminary phase. It does have a significance of its own. But the process of evangelism and nurture cannot be said to have reached its culmination until the junior soldier enters into adult commitment to Christian discipleship as a senior soldier.

2. The Receptivity Principle

The Receptivity Principle, the 11th in the list, recognises that there are degrees of receptivity and resistance to the gospel between different groups of people, and within each person at different times, and that the most fruitful evangelism will be that which is targeted towards receptive groups or towards individuals who are passing through a receptive phase. It is also known as the white harvest principle, and the agricultural model suggested by Jesus helps our understanding of the principle. Crops go through three stages: green, ripe and rotten. Harvest is only effective at one of these stages, and what the principle suggests is that within the overall priority of evangelism there should be the specific priority of concentrating our resources on those parts of the field which are already 'white unto harvest'. It can be stated as follows: *To grow, a corps must concentrate its evangelistic resources on those most receptive to the gospel.*

Like a number of other church growth principles, if pressed too far it becomes controversial. The Christian witness to everyone must be maintained. Seed that perhaps will bear fruit in the distant future must continue to be sown. But as the resources at our disposal are limited it is reasonable to target our main efforts towards those who are most ready to receive the message, and thus 'winning the winnable while they are winnable', as McGavran has put it.

Considerable research has been undertaken into the subject of Resistance and Receptivity, and a simple horizontal graph line is used to indicate the degree of negative or positive response to the message by groups or individuals. With the 'indifferent', shown usually by the figure 'O', in the middle of the line, the resistant shade off to the left in ever-increasing opposition, and the receptive shade off to the right in openness to the gospel. This is known as the Resistance-Receptivity Axis, and mentions of 'left end' and 'right end' people refer to this graph.

Another way of looking graphically at differing stages of receptivity within an individual has been developed by Dr James Engel and is therefore known as the 'Engel Scale'. Engel sees individuals as being placed somewhere on the following scale with regard to their spiritual awareness:

−10	Awareness of the supernatural
− 9	No effective knowledge of Christianity
− 8	Initial awareness of Christianity
− 7	Interest in Christianity
− 6	Awareness of basic facts of the gospel
− 5	Grasp of implications of the gospel
− 4	Positive attitude to the gospel
− 3	Awareness of personal need
− 2	Challenge and decision to act
− 1	Repentance and faith
0	A new disciple is born
+ 1	Evaluation of decision
+ 2	Initiation into the church

This model has its critics, but as long as it is kept in mind that no one *has* to pass through all the minor stages as separate stages, and that it is quite possible to go in an instant from − 10 to 0 in response to the gospel, the scale does provide a continual reminder that people are often at different levels in their spiritual awareness and that we need to start where they are. Sensitivity to the degree of receptivity of an individual has always been part of a soul-winner's secret.

To meet some of these criticisms the Engel scale has been modified by the Fuller Institute and the revision adds further insights. (See page 63).

Another aspect of research has been to try to identify factors that make for increased receptivity. For someone to have a personal link with a committed Christian is a most potent factor, as is a personal link with someone who is himself moving toward Christ (often leading to whole families becoming converted). A present or previous link with a church increases receptivity. There are also seasonal factors. People are more responsive at particular times of the year such as Christmas and Easter. There are age factors. Most conversions take place before the age of 30 or after the age of 60. The fewest conversions occur

MODIFIED ENGEL SCALE

DISCIPLESHIP: THE TOTAL PROCESS

PHASE I: MAKING DISCIPLES

		Original Engel Scale
STAGE 1	IGNORANCE OF CHRISTIANITY (May be exposed but pays no attention)	− 10 − 9
STAGE 2	AWARENESS OF CHRISTIANITY (Christianity is a religious option)	− 8 − 7
STAGE 3	UNDERSTANDING (What being a Christian implies)	− 6 − 5
STAGE 4	PERSONAL INVOLVEMENT (What Christ could do for me)	− 4 − 3
STAGE 5	DECISION (verdict) (I want it or I don't want it)	− 2 − 1
STAGE 6	REGENERATION (Disciple made—theologically)	0 + 1
STAGE 7	INCORPORATION (Disciple counted— strategically)	+ 2

PHASE II: TRAINING DISCIPLES + etc

in the 30-45 age group. There are need factors. The most responsive people of all are new people who seek out the corps and come to a meeting. In most cases it is some deep-seated need that has brought them there.

A significant result of such research is the finding that people are particularly responsive to the gospel when going through a period of transition. A period of transition 'is a span of time when a person's or a family's normal, everyday behaviour patterns are disrupted by some event that puts them into an unfamiliar situation'. The more such events in a person's life, the greater the receptivity to the Christian message.

In the 'Holmes and Rahe Social Readjustment Rating Scale' different categories of psychological stress which produce periods of transition have been categorised on a scale from 100 downwards. The higher the need rating for social readjustments, the greater the receptivity to the gospel. Death of a spouse has the highest rating at 100. This is followed by divorce with a rating of 73. Personal injury or illness rates 53, and so on. Some other events mentioned include marriage, unemployment, retirement, pregnancy, addition to the family, change of job, financial worries, son or daughter leaving home, starting or finishing school, change in working hours or conditions, moving house, even change in eating habits!

The importance of the 'rites of passage'—birth, puberty, adulthood, marriage, birth of children, death of loved ones, and dying—in the evangelistic mission has always been recognised. What church growth research is emphasising is that there are other events of transition which will also increase receptivity to Christ. The challenge is to seek to identify groups or individuals who are going through a period of transition, for to grow, a corps must concentrate its evangelistic resources on those most receptive to the gospel.

3. The Pragmatic Principle

Another crucial growth principle relating to evangelism is the Pragmatic Principle, the 12th in our list. Pragmatism is belief in what works. When applied to evangelism it refers only to the *methods* employed, not the content of the message or anything else, and must include the safeguard that no unworthy methods will be considered. What it means is that we are prepared to be 'ruthless in evaluating results' when it comes to our evangelistic methods, and to adapt, experiment and change until we discover methods that bring actual results, and then use those. Growing churches use evangelistic methods that work! We therefore arrive at the growth principle which reads: *To grow, a corps must use the evangelistic methods most calculated to achieve the aim of making soldier-disciples.*

William Booth was the supreme pragmatist when it came to evangelistic methodology. He also had a premonition of what might happen to the movement he had founded. 'The Army, by its very success, is ever in danger of drifting away from the great ungodly mass for whose salvation it was expressly raised up,' he warned. 'The gulf must be crossed and recrossed and crossed again. To overcome there must be skilful, persevering, systematic, desperate aggression. We must go to the people. *New methods must be invented if the old ones do not bring us into contact with these godless crowds.*'

William Booth foresaw the danger of the Army becoming separated from its own kind of people by the 'redemption and lift' phenomenon which church growth has identified. As people's lives and life-styles are changed through redemption the resulting socio-economic lift can actually hinder their evangelistic effectiveness. But more than that, William Booth foresaw the danger of the Army settling into a particular rut of evangelistic methodology, the danger of doing for doing's sake, of doing what has always been done regardless of whether it is effective or relevant, the danger of the means becoming the end. The Pragmatic Principle is all about 'skilful, persevering, systematic, desperate' outreach. Its heart is that 'new methods must be invented if the old ones do not bring us into contact' with those who need Christ.

Church growth thinking deals with general principles and does not specify particular evangelistic methods. Each church must discover what is right for it, and do whatever it can do well. Among the churches that are growing there is a wide diversity of evangelistic methodology. Some emphasise preaching, some house groups, some the large 'celebration' type of service, some make a special feature of music, while others stress visitation, or the adult Sunday-school or family services. There is no one method that is right for all situations.

Growing churches experiment and learn from their experiences. Not like the pastor, quoted by Monica Hill, who reported that he had mobilised his people to knock on doors with Christian literature. In three months they knocked on 2,000 doors. 'What was the response?' inquired Monica Hill. 'How many meaningful contacts did you make?' 'None,' replied the pastor, 'so we are going to redouble our efforts. We will knock on 4,000 doors next quarter'.

The Pragmatic Principle is, of course, explosive. It is sheer dynamite. For if applied too literally or foolishly there is a danger that in a declining situation—where the evangelistic methods being used are self-evidently not producing results—there could be a temptation to stop everything that is being attempted and try to start from scratch! That would be folly for any church, and more so in an Army which has a certain coherence and tradition of strategy. The Pragmatic Principle therefore needs to be tempered by the insight that not all evangelism comes in the Persuasion category. Presence and Proclamation evangelism also have their places.

ARRIVING AT A STRATEGY FOR GROWTH

Having considered evangelism from a number of angles and looked at three key growth principles, it will now be helpful to try to bring together all that has gone before and seek to arrive at a strategy for growth that will be applicable to corps of all sizes. Any such strategy must be comprehensive, taking in all aspects of corps life, and it must be permanent. Church growth, as already noted, is not an event, and neither is it a campaign or a programme. For the Army it is a re-call to that permanent set of attitudes which in our earlier days made every aspect of corps life evangelistic. Having looked at the three principles we can say that our evangelistic aim is clear—to make new soldier disciples. It is also clear that we need to concentrate our resources on the most receptive. With regard to methods we are prepared to be pragmatic.

If we are to reach out to the most receptive, the first step must be to seek to *identify* who they are. Having identified them, the second step must be to *cultivate* them, to reach out to them through regular contact and friendship. These two points will be considered under the heading 'Reaching out for growth' in chapter 5.

The next step must be to seek to *assimilate* these contacts into the life of the corps through activities, meetings, groups that are appropriate to them and which meet their needs. The fourth step will be to *nurture* them spiritually to the point of accepting Christ and then beyond to active soldiership and continual spiritual growth. These two steps will be the theme of chapter 6, 'Folding in for Growth', a title which avails itself of a useful pastoral term rich in meaning, popularised by church growth.

The initial letters of the four steps spell out *I CAN*, and we are indebted to the USA Western Territory for the inspiration of marshalling the appropriate church growth concepts under these headings and thus providing an easily remembered strategic pattern. It should be noted that cultivating, assimilating and nurturing often shade into each other, and that just as 'come' and 'go' structures of evangelism often have no clear dividing line, so 'reaching out' and 'folding in' may also overlap.

For discussion

1. Analyse the evangelistic activities of the corps in the light of the various ways mentioned of looking at evangelism.

2. What are the practical implications for the corps of the Soldier-Disciple Principle?

3. What are the practical implications for the corps of the Receptivity Principle?

4. What are the practical implications for the corps of the Pragmatic Principle?

5
Reaching out for growth

The first step in reaching out to those most responsive to the message is to identify them. This needs to be done in a methodical way. The aim must be to develop and maintain a *prospect list*, a list of people known by name and known well enough for the appropriate means of cultivation and assimilation to be determined according to their interests and needs. A prospect list is a vital part of a permanent strategy for it allows corps events and activities to be directed towards specific people, helps to identify bridges (another important church growth term) between people in the corps and these individuals, and helps to focus prayer on particular people.

IDENTIFYING THE MOST RECEPTIVE

Where are names to come from for the prospect list? There are three widely inclusive groups of people. Those that are receptive through having a personal link with a member of the corps, those that are receptive because they have a past or present link with the activities of the corps, and those that are receptive through what we might call heightened spiritual awareness, a spiritual sensitivity often prompted by sociological factors. The first two groups are people known by *name*. The third group are people who initially are *not* known by name.

1. The receptive—through personal links

Perhaps the most crucial piece of information referred to thus far is the poll result which indicated that as high a percentage as 75-90 per cent of new people who came to Christ did so because of a link with a friend or relative. Only a comparatively small percentage—10 to 25 per cent—became Christians because of the multitude of meetings, events, activities, drives and campaigns we normally associate with evangelism. These, as will be seen, are an important part of the overall strategy. But they are not the key factor. The key factor which emerged in this poll and which has been repeatedly confirmed by experience is that up to 90 per cent of those who become committed Christians do so because of a personal link with someone already within the church. For our purpose this means that the most receptive group of people by far are those who can be reached through personal links with members of the corps.

Dr Donald McGavran has drawn attention to the importance for evangelism of what he calls Web Movements. Through the web of inter-personal relationships, often diversifying in quite unexpected directions, the conversion of one leads to the conversion of many. On a still grander scale come the People Movements, when whole peoples turn to Christ, not merely in an outward formal way but because a series of 'multi-individual, mutually interdependent' decisions are made. Though People Movements occur almost exclusively on the mission field, extensive Web Movements have been noted in rapidly growing churches. They are, after all, but the outworking of the old principle of you bringing the one next to you and I bringing the one next to me!

An important point to note is that 'bringing' someone into the Christian fellowship through a personal relationship does not necessarily mean actually leading them to a point of decision and to Christ. Often the initial linking is very low key. It can be giving a friend a ticket for a special festival or suggesting they might like to come on a corps outing. Once the link has been made, all the influences of the Christian fellowship and the Christian message become operative.

'All Christians at all times,' comments Peter Wagner, 'should be prepared for that moment when God brings them into contact with a person prepared by the Holy Spirit for accepting Christ. And they should know how to introduce that person to Christ.' But in the Body of Christ there are those with special gifts for leading others into faith, and frequently it is the people with special evangelistic and counselling skills who are used by God at the moment of decision. All salvationists, however, are called to share their faith, all are called to 'bring', for without the initial link there can be no moment of salvation.

The importance of personal links in outreach is enshrined in the 13th principle, the Personal Link Principle, which is in the nature of an application of the Receptivity Principle: *To grow, a corps needs to reach out to those who are receptive through having personal links with members of the corps.* This principle is sometimes spoken of in terms of 'relational circles', 'areas of influence' or 'evangelistic potential' (EP).

Everyone stands in the centre of at least six circles of personal relationships or areas of influence. In most of these circles there will be people who are not committed Christians. Writing down the names of potential contacts in the various circles reveals the evangelistic potential (EP) of each salvationist. This can be surprisingly high. As a rule of thumb it is reckoned that most Christians have personal links of some kind or other with at least 100 uncommitted people. Adding together the individual EP of each member of the corps gives the total EP for the corps. If one takes the suggested average of 100 per person as a guide, it means that a corps with 50 members has an EP of 5,000 and one with 100 members a potential of 10,000. Quite some pool to fish in!

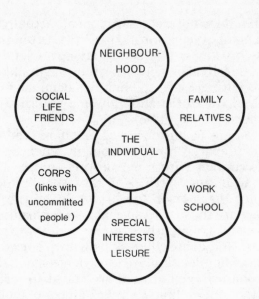

There is a curious factor at work, however, that needs mentioning. The longer a person has been a Christian, the lower his EP through relational circles! The shorter the time he has been saved, the higher his EP! The reason is simple. As we move into the Christian fellowship we increasingly spend our time and make our friends within it. After some years it is possible for a Christian to have few social contacts which are not already within the Christian ambit. A new convert, on the other hand, has most of his social contacts outside the Christian circle and therefore has a much bigger EP. For the first two or three years following conversion his EP is likely to be well in excess of the average 100, but after that it begins to fall. The greatest potential for evangelism through personal links lies therefore with new converts. Gaining just *one* new convert can set off a web movement of quite amazing dimensions, and at any point other web movements, leading in quite different directions, may be triggered off.

The actual names of individuals representing the EP of members of the corps is in one sense a very personal matter. The responsibility of each salvationist for personal reaching out to others will need to be a matter of continual teaching and continual prayer. But it becomes a corporate matter when salvationists are willing to share particular names for inclusion in the prospect list. Entries would need to include reference to them being personal prospects of particular salvationists as in most cases they would not be known to the corps. These names then become the object of intensive prayer and the group as a whole is able to offer encouragement and support to these personal endeavours. Prayer for soul-winning, prayer for growth, becomes far more significant and potent when it is focused in this way.

Considering that up to 90 per cent of new converts come from this particular group—those that have a personal link with a member of the corps—one might even question the need to look at other groups. But there is a second group of people who are also very receptive. They are people who already have a link, or had in the past, with the activities of the corps. The emphasis here is not so much on the personal web of relationships which each salvationist has, as on the web of relationships which are set up through the activities of the corps. Uncommitted parents of children who attend juniors, and former juniors who once attended the corps, are examples of such relationships present and past. It needs to be stressed, however, that even these activity-based relationships usually have a strong personal relationship factor. People do not so much have a relationship with a corps in abstract as with particular people within it whom they get to know through the activities. It is therefore highly likely that a good number of the 90 per cent already mentioned had their friendship link formed with a church member through the activities of that church. Let's now look at this second group of highly receptive people.

2. The receptive—through corps links

A useful way of looking at a corps is to picture it as three circles within one: the salvationist circle, the fellowship circle and the mission circle. The salvationist circle represents the core of committed and active people within the corps. The second circle represents the people who are more at the fringe of things, ranging from the regular, but uncommitted, attenders at meetings to husbands of home league members who might occasionally show some interest. The third circle represents the community as a whole, those the corps must seek to reach out to but who as yet are not within even the outer borders of the corps fellowship. Giving the circles the colours red, green and grey respectively, we can say that the evangelistic aim of the corps must be to seek to expand the red circle into the green area, and to expand the green circle into the grey. The great strength of this model is its open-endedness. Showing the outer circle as the community beyond the corps acts as a continual reminder that no corps or church can sit back until all the 'grey' within their reach has become 'green' on its way to becoming 'red'. That is what is known as 'winning the world for Jesus'!

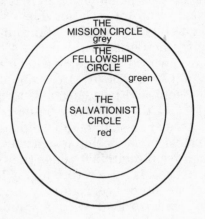

Using this helpful model of a corps we can say that the second group of receptive people we are now considering are those in the green area, those who are already within the fellowship of the corps in its widest sense. In other words, people who already have some link with the corps and are known by name.

This is such an essential aspect of outreach that it merits being stated in the form of a principle. The Corps Link Principle (number 14) reads: *To grow a corps needs to reach out to those who are receptive through having past or present links with the activities of the corps.*

With the help of corps records and drawing on the personal knowledge of salvationists about corps contacts past and present, it is usually possible to add—and keep adding—a considerable number of names to the prospect list from this group. Sources from which new senior soldiers might come range from just within the green circle to almost touching the grey, and include:

- [ ] Ex-soldiers
- [ ] Adherents

- [ ] Recruits
- [ ] YP recruits

- [ ] Converts
- [ ] Regular Sunday attenders
- [ ] Former attenders
- [ ] Visitors in meetings
- [ ] Outpost contacts

- [ ] Home fellowship contacts
- [ ] Home league members
- [ ] Families of HL members

- [ ] Home league fellowship members
- [ ] Families of home league fellowship members

- [ ] Former HL and HL fellowship members

- [ ] Over-60 club members

- [ ] Families of over-60s
- [ ] Children dedicated
- [ ] Parents of children dedicated
- [ ] Cradle roll parents
- [ ] Play group parents
- [ ] Families on YP roll

- [ ] Ex-YP roll and families
- [ ] Ex-junior soldiers

- [ ] Families of YP attending week-night activities
- [ ] Youth club members
- [ ] Youth fellowship members
- [ ] Young people who attend Sunday meetings
- [ ] Families of young adults
- [ ] Spouses of salvationists
- [ ] Relatives associated with funerals
- [ ] People married in the Army

- [ ] Donors

- [ ] Charity shop contacts

- [ ] People known through other corps activities
- [ ] People known through use of corps buildings
- [ ] Community service recipients
- [ ] Coffee morning contacts
- [ ] League of mercy contacts

- [ ] Pub-booming contacts
- [ ] Open-air meeting contacts
- [ ] Visitation contacts
- [ ] Ministry to eventide homes contacts
- [ ] Ministry to hospitals contacts
- [ ] Unchurched friends in the community

Adding specific names from these sources to those

provided by salvationists from their own personal relational circle will create an extensive prospect list in even the smallest corps. But there is a third source yet to be considered.

3. The receptive—through heightened spiritual awareness

In this category come people who initially are *not known by name* but who are receptive through heightened spiritual awareness, prompted directly by the Holy Spirit or indirectly through sociological factors. It is a fundamental tenet of Christian doctrine that the Holy Spirit is always at work in people's lives. Within every community there will therefore be those who at any given time have reached a point of special spiritual sensitivity. Sociological factors, as was previously noted, such as undergoing a period of transition, often make people more spiritually aware and open to the work of the Spirit. As this category of people is amply covered by the Receptivity Principle there is no need to include them in another growth principle as such, but the big question is how to identify by name people within this group. Two points ought to be made in this connection.

Firstly, in all outreach activities the corps folk need to make it their initial goal to identify people who are spiritually sensitive and to establish personal links with these particular individuals by name. Many Presence and Proclamation evangelistic endeavours would enter the coveted Persuasion bracket simply by giving them a sharper focus on the goal of establishing vital links with individuals. Much evangelism is of necessity to the who-soever, the passer-by, the stumbler across treasure. There will always be an element of scattering the seed at random. Open-air meetings, door-to-door visitation, pub-booming, hospital ministry, and similar evangelistic ventures come in this category. But the secret lies in seeing these activities as providing a vehicle for the fulfilment of the key preliminary aim, which is to identify and forge a personal link with individuals who for any reason are spiritually sensitive at that point in time.

Secondly, there needs to be an awareness and sensitivity on the part of all who engage in evangelistic work to the factors which make for increased spiritual openness in people. This is not only a matter of praying for great spiritual perceptiveness. It is also a question of learning from the sociological disciplines. The salvationist will therefore be at his most sensitive when in the course of his evangelistic activities he comes across people who are passing through a period of transition. He will recognise that when a person's everyday behaviour pattern has been disrupted, by events ranging from the trauma of the loss of a loved one or other personal tragedy, to the more mundane transitions like moving into a new neighbourhood, he will be particularly open to spiritual influences. The identification of individuals who are receptive in this way is a process which can and ought to go well beyond the usual evangelistic activities of the corps. Knowledge of the community through radio, local newspapers and word of mouth will bring to the attention of the corps, individuals who are likely to be particularly receptive and whose names can be added to the prospect list. Times of special evangelistic emphasis, such as campaigns, will also provide further prospects.

The PALS System

The Australian territories have formalised the concept of drawing names from the three sources mentioned for inclusion in a prospect list, into a comprehensive framework known as the PALS System, The People Already Linked System. Its five-fold purpose is:

1. To introduce people to Jesus Christ as Lord and Saviour.
2. To assimilate people already loosely linked into the full fellowship of the local corps.
3. To build bridges of love and concern between salvationists and people within the Army network.
4. To encourage people to make The Salvation Army their church.

5. To enlist people in the service of the local corps and utilise their skills in the interest of the community.

Salvationists are invited to submit names for the PALS list and can offer to become the 'carer' for particular people. The list is sub-divided into categories by source (eg, regular charity shop customers, people dedicated in The Salvation Army, etc) and names are continually added and each name periodically reviewed. PALS go on the mailing list of the corps and receive regular news about special events. Through a network of 'carers' they are regularly kept in touch with through phone calls or visits. They become the object of focused prayer.

By every means possible it is sought to assimilate them into the life of the corps as a first step towards them becoming soldier-disciples of Christ. Lists under such headings as *120 ways to gain new PALS* and *60 ways to involve our PALS*—from which points have been drawn for both the preceding and following section of this book—stimulate both the process of how to identify and how to cultivate the most receptive. It is now to this second part of the process that we turn.

CULTIVATING THE MOST RECEPTIVE

Having identified the receptive it is now a matter of cultivating these contacts in the working out of the I CAN strategy. The idea of strengthening initial personal links in this way stands in time-honoured tradition. One of the greatest corps officers of all time in Britain was Major Jack Stoker. He was a soul-winner on the grand scale. At Monkwearmouth, Sunderland, so many drunks got converted that 13 public houses had to close down within three months of his arrival in town. One hundred and twenty converts were gained on one Sunday alone. And when the stonelaying for the new hall took place, 3,000 people sat down for a public tea and the shipyards and works had to allow a holiday for the occasion.

Jack Stoker knew how to cultivate people for Christ. The announcement of his promotion to Glory set off a train of memories: 'At Chester-le-Street they remembered how he arrived in the town and before he was known to anyone there had squatted down among some miners who were sitting around the pithead. "You've some very fair dogs here," he said. "Can they run any?" And the men fell to talking about the prowess of their pets. Then he took them over to a temperance hotel and stood them all drinks of ginger ale. Never a word of salvation he spoke—only dogs and ginger ale. "Know who he was?" someone asked the men after he had gone. "That's the leader of the mission." That night the building was absolutely packed with men and their dogs, and Stoker talked to them from eight till nearly 10 with never a break for singing or prayer.

'In another town a man remembered his conversion. Irreligious and blasphemous, he had assured his salvationist wife that he would break the neck of any Army officer who dared set foot in his house. But he had been helpless and surprised when Stoker, rushing in one day, stood for a moment or two in front of a cage in which a canary was singing blithely, and exclaimed emphatically, "My, yon's a bird any man could be proud of!" and then apologising for his bad manners hurried out again. Next time he saw Stoker, he asked: "So you like birds, do you, captain?" but Stoker, while declaring that he almost worshipped them, had added that he was quite unable to stay that day to discuss them. At the next meeting, however, the man's wife announced: "My husband says you're the only Salvation Army officer that's ever been sent to this town who's got brains. You've got to come to tea on Sunday!" Stoker went, but did not say grace or mention religion. He was invited again and talked dogs, horses, birds, sports of every kind, but no religion. By about the sixth visit he got as far as telling the bird fancier some of the experiences of his early days. Suddenly he put his hand on the man's shoulder and added, earnestly, "But God has saved me from all that and made me a soul-winner. And if you will cry to God he will do for you what he has done for me." The man had fallen to his knees and sought God's forgiveness, and now, at the time of Stoker's passing was a well-known local officer in The Salvation Army's ranks.'

It needs to be mentioned once more that the phases of cultivating and assimilating and nurturing flow into each other and cannot always be clearly distinguished. The fact that the initial letters form the one word CAN, whereas the I stands separate, acts as a reminder about this.

If the identification homework has been done well, even the smallest corps is likely to have a fairly long list of prospects. The ability to keep in some kind of contact with them all is important but will often depend on the resources available. Within the priority of the receptive, however, there will need to be a further priority, a special focus on those that are whitest unto harvest. Often a chain of conversions has started by a group as a whole concentrating their faith and prayer and effort on just *one* individual! That is, of course, extreme—but so would the opposite be of trying to win everyone at once.

From those receptive through personal links with corps members, each salvationist will need to seek to strengthen the ties with those within his or her relational circle who at that time show the greatest signs of being receptive. From those receptive through personal links with corps activities, it will be a matter of the salvationists with the greatest personal affinity seeking to establish the relationship further. Affinity can depend on such factors as age, sex, special interests held in common, past association in the corps, friendship, work, etc. From the list of contacts established through evangelistic activities and community awareness it will depend on affinity and availability as to who follows up whom. Salvationists who live far away from the corps will find it harder to draw people to it from their personal relational circles and may therefore wish to give increased time to the cultivation of contacts in the second and third category. For both salvationists personally and the corps as a whole the continual strategy needs to be to win the most winnable first through those who have the closest affinity.

The aim is to strengthen the relationship that has been established and to draw the person to Christ by bringing him into contact with that aspect of corps life which is most likely to interest, influence and finally persuade him. Hard sell can prove counter-productive. Too much emphasis too soon on commitment has been found to reap results in terms of decisions, but to yield little by way of long-term discipling. A church growth survey of active church members found that on average they had been exposed to 'religious events' 5.8 times before making a well thought-out, conscious decision. This is probably paralleled in the experience of most first generation salvationists. The first aim must therefore be to make and develop friendships. From that will follow naturally the further assimilation into the life of the corps.

Establishing and cultivating friendship links can be done in innumerable ways big and small. Here are some suggestions:

- ☐ Invite them to corps special events
- ☐ Invite them to corps social or recreational events
- ☐ Give them an appropriate book or pamphlet to read
- ☐ Take them to a large SA event
- ☐ Pray for them
- ☐ Invite them home for a meal
- ☐ Arrange for corps activities to be held in their home
- ☐ Invite them to an appropriate home group
- ☐ Invite them to an appropriate group which meets at the hall
- ☐ Visit them regularly—'short and sweet' calls
- ☐ Link them up with any salvationists living nearby
- ☐ If necessary, create new groups to match their interests
- ☐ Arrange for them to receive SA literature
- ☐ Involve them and use their skills in league of mercy and other corps activities
- ☐ Arrange special events at the corps tailored to their interests
- ☐ Telephone regularly
- ☐ Write a letter from time to time
- ☐ Ensure they are on the corps mailing list
- ☐ Celebrate their special occasions: birthdays, anniversaries, etc
- ☐ Arrange for transport to corps

- [ ] Take every opportunity of introducing them to other corps members
- [ ] Ensure they have been included on the corps prayer list
- [ ] Provide a free Bible at the appropriate time
- [ ] Follow up quickly when they are ill or distressed
- [ ] Involve them in your own personal special occasions like birthdays, etc
- [ ] Arrange babysitting if necessary to allow them to attend the meetings
- [ ] Discover and seek to meet their needs
- [ ] Talk up your corps—be positive
- [ ] Make them feel wanted—that they belong
- [ ] Listen to them—ask for their advice regarding corps and personal matters
- [ ] Share your faith informally with them, let them sense what Jesus means to you
- [ ] Love them in Jesus' name!

We have now reached the point where 'reaching out' begins to blend with 'folding in'. A number of the ideas mentioned above depend not only on personal cultivation of a relationship but on there being adequate arrangements for assimilation and nurture within the life of the corps. One of the very significant emphases of church growth is its stress on the importance of smaller groups and activities within the church as a whole. When such groups and activities are 'open' they act as points of entry. Groups also play a crucial role in the assimilation and holding of newcomers and in the nurture of new members in the faith. A comprehensive evangelistic strategy must therefore include the provision of as many 'entry' and 'holding' points within the corps structure as possible.

The importance of small groupings within the larger unit is not a new discovery but rather a rediscovery of what has been known since the days of the Early Church. Apart from the Temple in Jerusalem in the very early stages there simply were no large buildings available to Christians. They therefore met in their homes as a matter of course and occasionally got together in larger units as and when they could. John Wesley divided his methodist societies into classes and bands, every member of the church being a member of a class which met weekly in a home, usually on a week-night, and some being a member of a band as well. 'The class meeting became the primary means of grace for thousands of methodists,' writes Howard E. Snyder. 'It served an evangelistic and discipling function.' The class was an 'open' group and most conversions occurred in the classes rather than in the Sunday services when all the classes came together. The bands were smaller 'closed' groups for the instruction of believers.

It was only natural that William Booth would transfer this methodist heritage to The Salvation Army. On the pastoral side the 1886 edition of *Orders and Regulations for Field Officers* outlines the ward system with visitation sergeants responsible for the welfare of not more than 12 other salvationists—but rising to 24 or a maximum of 36 if assisted by one or two corporals respectively. Incidentally, they were to mark their guard books with the following marks 'to indicate the various conditions of the soldiers':

E —an efficient soldier
G —in good spiritual condition
A —absent from most open-air meetings without good reasons

U —unwell
C —growing cold
B —backslider
D —deserted his colours
O —out of town

On the functional side salvationists were divided into brigades. The 1886 edition lists the following brigades as 'at present at work'. The list should help to dispel any notion that community service is a recent addition to corps life:

- [ ] Rescue brigades
- [ ] *War Cry* brigades
- [ ] Prison-gate brigades
- [ ] Cellar, gutter and garret brigades
- [ ] Drunkards' brigades
- [ ] Workhouse brigades
- [ ] Lodging-house brigades
- [ ] Nursing brigades
- [ ] Little soldiers' brigades
- [ ] Outpost brigades
- [ ] Public-house brigades

In later editions of the *Orders and Regulations* the concept of the corps being divided into brigades was further developed. Until as recently as 1976 it was laid down that all corps with over 150 soldiers *had* to operate the brigade system and that smaller corps should adopt it *as far as possible.*

'To be effective,' the book stated, 'this system must embrace *every individual* in the corps, providing for each spiritual oversight and suitable salvation employment.' The brigades were divided into two categories: 'special service brigades', like those listed above, and 'corps brigades' which consisted of the sections which make up corps life. The leaders were known as brigade leaders, unless they had some other official title like bandmaster or home league secretary which in those cases superseded their brigade leader titles. Great latitude appears to have been granted to the corps officer under the watchful eye of the divisional commander for the creation of different kinds of brigades according to shared interests and circumstances. A list of the brigades mentioned in the course of the relevant chapter is instructive:

- ☐ Band
- ☐ Songster brigade
- ☐ YP workers' brigade
- ☐ Corps cadet brigade
- ☐ Recruits and converts' brigade
- ☐ Brothers' brigade
- ☐ Sisters' brigade
- ☐ Home league brigade (for soldier members)
- ☐ Heralds' brigade
- ☐ Bandsmen's wives brigade
- ☐ Veterans' brigade
- ☐ District brigade
- ☐ Visitation brigade

(the latter two to be subdivided into marrieds and singles if too large)

The important points to notice are the recognition of the need for smaller groupings and for flexibility. But as this is not a history book it is now a matter of seeing how the principle of small groups within the larger unit—on which the behavioural sciences have shed so much light in recent years—can be used to *assimilate* and *nurture* the receptive in the I CAN strategy.

For discussion

1. How can salvationists be further encouraged to reach out to the receptive, known by name, who stand within their personal relational circles?
2. How do the 'red' and 'green' areas of the corps compare for size, and how can the corps more methodically identify and cultivate the receptive, known by name, in the green area?
3. How can the corps better identify and cultivate the receptive, not known by name, who for a variety of reasons might be specially open to the gospel?

6
Folding in for growth

The term 'folding in' means much more than simply bringing the sheep within the fold. It has the underlying connotation of the sheep settling in their new environment and being fed and being content. Church growth recognises that in many ways it is the point of incorporation, of assimilation, of 'folding in' that is the most vital in the evangelistic process. Following assimilation, and often concurrently, comes nurture which also includes shepherding. At any point in this process can come the decision of commitment to Christ, and everything must first lead towards that moment, and when it has happened lead away from it to further nurture, further learning, further commitment, further service, as the person prepares to become a soldier-disciple and begins to live and work as one.

ASSIMILATION AND NURTURE OF THE RECEPTIVE

Having *identified* the most receptive and *cultivated* those most ready to respond, as part of the I CAN strategy, it is now a matter of considering how the last two points of that strategy can best be worked out in practice: the need to *assimilate* and to *nurture.*

1. Assimilating the receptive

The I CAN material develops these points as follows:
'Assimilation involves determining how the corps might fold in the contact with the corps as a whole in its Sunday meetings, and also with an appropriate "nurture and fellowship" or "task and fellowship" group. Unless the corps is very small, it is difficult for a new person to relate with the total corps at once. A new person needs to relate first with a smaller grouping within the whole, a grouping in which he feels comfortable and which meets his needs. Groups which meet the needs of Christians do not necessarily meet the needs of non-Christians and careful thought must therefore be given to the needs of each individual. Assimilation is *not* automatic, it takes conscious effort and the responsibility for seeing it happens rests with the corps, not the newcomer. Ideally it will have started in the *cultivation* stage, so that the transition into the corps is natural and easy.'

'Commitment grows by involvement, and care is expressed for the newcomer by providing a meaningful place of involvement in the fellowship. The quicker the response by opening up such opportunities, the sooner will the sense of caring be communicated. Let newcomers participate! This might be by involving them in a

☐ *Task* — An assignment such as helping to plan a meeting, or participating in one in a special way, or working on a project;

☐ *Role* — A position on a task force, leadership of an informal group, member of a welcoming team;

☐ *Group*— A group appropriate to their interests and needs.'

'It is a documented fact that unless a new member makes a number of friends in the first six months he will drop out. The strategy needs to take account of this.'

INTERNATIONAL
LIBRARY
TRAINING COLLEGE

2. Nurturing the receptive

'Nurturing involves teaching, leading to Christ, discipling and equipping for ministry. The aim is to develop committed Christians with the willingness and ability to reproduce themselves. This will include teaching them about prayer, Bible study, testimony, personal giving; and the discovery, development and use of spiritual gifts, the stewardship of time, how to witness, and how to care for others.'

'Shepherding is an essential part of nurturing, and a system needs to be developed whereby the "back door" of the corps is in effect closed. Through lack of such a system, some corps lose more through the back door than they gain through the front! 'Shepherding is not just the officer's task—salvationists in the corps may have this gift and if so must use it. The shepherding system devised will ensure that any signs of inactivity or hurt are noticed promptly and dealt with efficiently. The precautions will include, for example, provision for:

☐ Identifying newcomers to meetings and following them up.
☐ Identifying regular attenders who are absent for more than three or four weeks, and following them up.
☐ Identifying conflict and taking appropriate steps to resolve it.'

ASSIMILATION AND NURTURE THROUGH SMALLER GROUPS

The importance of smaller groups within the corps as a whole will by now have been established. According to Richard Peace, writing in *Small Group Evangelism* (Scripture Union), 'the Church "discovered" small groups in the 1950s and 60s'—though he recognises that it was a matter of rediscovery. 'In the late 1930s,' he writes, 'the scientific study of groups blossomed at the Kurt Lewin's Research Centre for Group Dynamics. Out of his work "group dynamics" emerged as a discipline in its own right.

The group dynamics movement has had a major impact on colleges, business and community groups of all sorts. Role playing, buzz sessions, T-groups, group therapy, brain-storming sessions, encounter groups and sensitivity training have become well known. Researchers have measured everything from group decision making to conflict resolution, and empathetic listening to leadership styles. Still, small groups were not widespread in the churches until the middle of this century. The discovery of their value seems to have been sparked by what social scientists were learning about groups. Suddenly church leaders began to speak of small groups in glowing terms.'

In his comprehensive study of home-based groups in *I Believe in Church Growth* (Hodder) Eddie Gibbs sees groups as being strategically important. First, because of their *intimacy* in an urban society which combines so many powerful depersonalising elements. Second, because of their *flexibility* in bringing together people from a variety of backgrounds. Third, because of the sense of *community* and fellowship they provide. And fourth, because of their *mobility*, with home-based cells enabling the church to multiply economically and speedily. He sees the purpose of groups as being sevenfold:

1. To provide a learning situation
2. To develop meaningful relationships
3. To identify gifts
4. To train new leaders
5. To ensure greater pastoral care
6. To demonstrate concern for the neighbourhood
7. To establish local bases for evangelism

In *Community in Mission* (International Headquarters) Phil Needham emphasises the importance of small groups within the corps. 'The small group can become a vehicle of encouragement because it can serve as a kind of extended family within the congregation: a place of personal belonging where certain needs are met, personal growth is nurtured, members are respected and loved and empathy is felt.'

In a recent Bible Society survey of *growing* churches it was discovered that 94 per cent of them had small groups meeting mainly in homes. But in considering ways of assimilating and nurturing newcomers and new members the small group phenomenon has to be considered as a whole. Groups do not only meet in homes. In fact the majority of them meet at the hall. In a sense a corps is a collection of groups. Some of the groups are made up exclusively of salvationists. They are the closed groups. Others are made up of salvationists and non-salvationists. They are the open groups. Sunday is the day when all the groups come together and the corps is seen as whole. It is rare, however, for all non-salvationist group members to choose to attend Sunday meetings, but a very special event might draw non-Army home league, over-60 club and youth club members and others in such numbers that the full picture of the corps becomes visible to the eye.

Returning now to a receptive person who has been *identified* and *cultivated* and who is wanting to become *assimilated* into a corps, we will picture him as a young man, and watch his attempted entry into Corps A below:

CORPS A

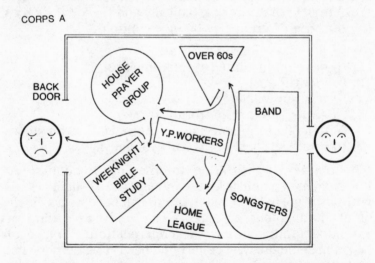

The first point to notice is the symbolic smallness of the front door and that there is only one way of entry. Then note as he approaches a group that appeals to him: the band. He discovers it is a closed group. You have to be a salvationist to belong. He then tries the songsters, with the same result. Having always been interested in youth work he tries to 'get in' to the YP workers' group on that basis. There should be opportunities for even uncommitted people to lend a hand with YP activities— provide transport and equipment, take groups out for activities—but the needed imagination on the part of the YP leaders in this case is missing and he is gently told to come back when he has become a uniformed salvationist. He then espies an 'open' group—hope at last! But it is the home league—and he is a man! Another open door beckons—but to belong you have to be over 60 and he is young. He hears about a house prayer group that meets in a home in a well-to-do suburb. Theoretically it is 'open' but as it is the same four couples who have met together for the last five years the group has become 'resistant' to new members. They seem too formidable as people for him to think of gatecrashing, and as none of them invite him or offer to come and fetch him, it is to all intents and purposes a closed group. Finally, however, he walks through the open door of the week-night Bible study held at the hall. The welcome is warm and genuine, but as everyone there is 50 or above, a life-long salvationist, and female, his enthusiasm begins to wane after a few weeks—and out he slinks through the big and wide-open back door.

Groups can be 'open/closed' or 'receptive/resistant' for a variety of reasons, some of which will have become obvious from the above illustration. To belong to some groups one has to be a salvationist, for others one has to have particular skills as well, like musical ability, for yet others one has to be a man, or a woman, or young, or old. But even if one scales all the qualification barriers there are other more subtle barriers to be overcome. Any group—even if theoretically an open one—which has been in operation with the same members for 18 months to two years is likely to be resistant to newcomers—though the members would vehemently deny it! Our friend didn't feel he could gatecrash the house prayer group for to him its members seemed too different—older, established

professional people. So there was a sociological barrier. Even the weeknight Bible study turned out to be not his kind of people, however warm their welcome.

Groups can become too inward-turned, they can unconsciously freeze out those who do not fit into a particular mould, and they can fail to cater for someone's interests in company with people with whom he feels at ease. There are many subtle factors at work. And assimilation refers not only to a newcomer arriving at a corps. There must also be scope for progressive assimilation as he becomes committed and becomes a uniformed salvationist—by which time his interests may have changed dramatically, thus adding to the factors at work.

Perhaps our young friend will do better as he approaches Corps B as a newcomer:

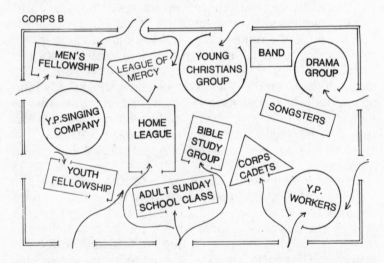

CORPS B

As Corps B happens to be a dream corps for any young man seeking entry he soon finds his niche and forgets about looking for the back door. In fact, seeing he has some musical knowledge, once he has become a soldier all the groups except the home league and the singing company will be open to him. The symbolism of the many doors of entry is important. In the cultivation, assimilation, nurturing cycle it is vital that there should be as many points of entry as possible. Many a salvationist has been won for Christ through a keep-fit class, by bringing her child to the play group, or by going to a social evening.

FOUR GROWTH PRINCIPLES RELATING TO ASSIMILATION AND NURTURE

Some of the points considered thus far come into the category of church growth principles, and we will look briefly at four of these.

First, the Multiple Entry Point Principle, number 15 on the list. *To grow, a corps needs to provide multiple entry points through its activities, meetings, groups and programmes in order to assimilate new people.* No corps can do everything, hold every type of meeting or engage in every type of activity. But it is a matter of multiplying the points of entry as far as the resources will allow—and then a little beyond that. The Sunday meetings are good points of entry, then there is the home league, then there are the various aspects of the YP corps, and then . . . what? That can only be answered by each corps individually. But a candid review of the current 'entry points' and their effectiveness, and any improvements or additions that might be made, is a useful exercise. How, and how soon, could a newcomer get involved in some way? That is the true test.

Second, the Multiple Holding Point Principle, number 16 on our list. *To grow, a corps needs to provide multiple holding points through its activities, meetings, groups and programmes in order to nurture, shepherd, train and use its new and existing people.* Again, every corps will have to work within its resources. But to picture our young friend arriving for the first time at the corps, and then to follow him through into soldiership, and to see with the mind's eye which groups would be open to him at the various stages, can be instructive. The same exercise should also be done with different categories of people in mind: a young woman, an older person, a family, and so on. How, and how soon, and for how long would a newcomer or new member find himself satisfyingly involved in some way? That is the true test of the effectiveness of our arrangements for assimilation and nurture.

Third, the Like Appreciates Like Principle, number 17 in our list. *To grow, a corps needs to establish as many points in common as it can with the people it is trying to reach.* The young man of our story felt he would be out of place at the prayer group because the people seemed forbidding, he felt ill-at-ease in the week night Bible study because he was the only young person there. He would have felt totally out of place in the home league. Why? Because there is a deep-seated desire within us all to be with people who are like ourselves. This deep-seated feeling was recognised by William Booth and his followers. They went out of their way to make people who felt uncomfortable and ill at ease in church feel comfortable and at ease in Army meetings. The friendly informality, the happy singing, the occasional laugh, the absence of church jargon, and especially the fact that so often it was someone like them leading and always some of their own testifying, made it seem more like the familiar music hall than St Mary's on the Hill.

McGavran recognised that people preferred to become Christians without having to cross social, cultural, linguistic or other barriers, and that led him to enunciate the now somewhat controversial homogenous unit (HU) principle—that like appreciates like. The fact that society as a whole and all churches everywhere divide into groups according to interest, age, sex, purpose—from golf clubs to trade unions, from schools to mothers' unions—is an indication of how fundamental to human nature the Like Appreciates Like Principle is. In fact when it comes to groups there can be no real quarrel with the homogenous unit principle. It is only when it is sought to be applied to a church or a corps as a whole, with the implied message that only our kind of people are welcome here, that it becomes controversial.

The Like Appreciates Like Principle does, however, present a challenge to many corps, especially where the previously mentioned 'redemption and lift' factor has been at work. If that has resulted in a migration to the suburbs one can have an inner city corps with no salvationists living nearby and with very little in common with the people who do. Because of the like appreciates like factor the sight of well-heeled salvationists emerging from their cars can prove extremely irritating to the local people. Perhaps only by caring community service, intelligently applied E-2 evangelism, and quick assimilation and promotion of new members from the locality to positions of leadership, can such a situation be rescued. However, the classic cameo of Lady Beatrice kneeling at the mercy seat with Dirty Jimmy, as described in *The Old Corps*, and saying to the officer, 'Leave him alone, captain, we're both seeking the same Lord', reminds us that the early Army could cope with socio/economic extremes. Homogenous unit principle or no, there is no reason why it should not do so today.

Fourth, the Meet Needs Principle, number 18 in the list. *To grow, a corps should seek to meet the needs of the people it is trying to reach and hold.* That great possibility thinker of church growth, Robert Schuller, put it in a nutshell when he said, 'The secret of success is to find a need and fill it.' The immensely successful Garden Grove Community Church in California represents the outworking of the dictum. As nobody *orders* anyone to church or Army on a Sunday—though a sense of duty might act as a spur—one can only conclude that if a church or corps is full to overflowing it is because that place of worship *is meeting the needs of those who belong.*

Those needs might be the need for meaningful and warm worship, or for fellowship, or for the sense of belonging to a community, or for sound Christian teaching, or for a desire to find an outlet for Christian service, or for the need to exercise gifts of the Spirit such as hospitality, teaching, leading, or simply for a good sing. Whatever the needs might be, the simple process of counting heads will tell us that they are being met at that particular church or corps. No amount of dragooning people by stern calls to Christian duty will make people come. But find a need and meet it—show them how in Christ and his fellowship their particular need can be met—and they will be there!

ASSIMILATION AND NURTURE THROUGH GROUP, CORPS AND CELEBRATION EVENTS

We must now look closer at the network of groups to be found in a Salvation Army corps. For the sake of completeness it will be necessary to study a fairly large corps, and allowance will have to be made for that when the principles are applied in smaller settings.

Of classifying of groups into categories and the giving of names to them in church growth thinking there is no end. Groups are classified according to membership, according to purpose, according to location, and according to size, subject matter, style, and much more, with names ranging from nutritive cells through accountability groups to spiritual kinship fellowships. Peter Wagner himself has given us the well-known formula:

$$Cell + Congregation + Celebration = Church$$

For all its neatness it is difficult to apply that formula to the Army setting. It seems to reflect something of the super churches. Wagner's use of the word congregation for what we would call a section, meeting, club, activity or fellowship can be confusing. Neither do we have an exact equivalent of a cell—a small group of 8-12 people. To us that is a 'small group', meeting for some particular purpose. Seeing the old Army 'in' word for groups and activities of all kinds—brigades—is now out, I propose to classify *all* the various events which make up corps life— meetings, clubs, fellowships, working parties, practices, parades, play groups, charity shops, league of mercy activities, etc—simply as *group events*, keeping the term *corps event* for when the groups come together, usually on a Sunday. The word *celebration* will be reserved for the big inter-corps, divisional, territorial and ecumenical events. So we have:

☐ Group events
☐ Corps events
☐ Celebration events

ASSIMILATION AND NURTURE THROUGH GROUP EVENTS

In considering the various activities and events which constitute the 'groups' within corps life, we will study their potential for both initial and continual assimilation and nurture, and also their potential as outreach groups.

Week-night meeting. The week-night meeting is a genuinely open group with potential for outreach, assimilation and nurture. The days of a meeting every night have gone, and so have the days of 'general' public meetings. Mid-week events need to be much more targeted, at specific subjects like Bible study, prayer, spiritual growth, and at specific groups of people like well-established Christians, new Christians, the young, the mature, etc, using the means of communication that will be most effective: teaching, studying, discussion, video, etc. They can be held at the hall or in a home, but if held in a home it is important that the open character is not lost. Any planning for growth needs to include plans for one or more week-night events tailor-made for those it is hoped to assimilate. More will be said on this subject under house groups.

Home league and home league fellowship. The home league and home league fellowship are not only open groups for women by definition, but also have an outreach mission written into their constitutions. Over the years they have had a successful record in reaching out to, and folding in new prospects. Many salvationists will testify to having walked initially through one of those two entry doors. The smaller the groups the greater the danger of them losing their absorbency and becoming resistant. The leadership needs to keep the Priority Principle always in its thinking. (To grow, a corps—and each group within it—must make evangelism its priority.) The evangelistic potential of the home league and the home league fellowship through its relational circles, is likely to be in treble figures. Creating a successful fellowship and even bringing in new members is only a mission completed in part. It is when home league members or members of their families get converted and move through to discipleship as Salvation Army soldiers that the full mission has been completed.

Over-60 club. The over-60 club also has potential for both outreach and assimilation/nurture, and has a fine record in this respect. Most of what has been said above regarding the home league has application here as well. The EP through relational circles is incalculable. The leadership needs to keep the Priority Principle in view throughout in order that the 'mission completed' stage may be reached with all who are receptive.

Youth club and youth fellowship. Both the week-night youth club and the Sunday evening youth fellowship have tremendous potential for outreach as well as initial assimilation and continual nurture. Opportunities for social fellowship and sport and fun ought to be integral parts of corps life, but if the leadership works to the Priority and Personal Link Principles both these events can become centres of youth evangelism and youth nurturing. The Christian youth club and youth fellowship are meant to give young people more than just a good time—they are meant to give them Christ.

Band and songsters. The Army's musical sections are the envy of the churches. They are one of our great strengths, with potential for both outreach and assimilation/nurture. Both the band and the songster brigades are task groups, groups knit together through being engaged in a common task. Part of that task, especially for the band, is to engage in Presence and Proclamation Evangelism in the open air. The effectiveness of this is greatly enhanced if accompanied by Persuasion Evangelism through door to door or street contacts by salvationists specially gifted for this type of work.

The surface has yet only been scratched with regard to the potential that the musical sections have for attracting and drawing PALS and the general public to special events as part of the I CAN process. Music is a universal language. One has only to think how pervasive it is throughout the day in the life of the average individual. It is a matter of getting the dialect right, however, and getting the right music targeted at the right group.

As far as assimilation of newcomers is concerned the musical sections have the double barriers of a skill to be learnt and commitment as a soldier to be made. Surprisingly, the Army has not been as quick as other churches with less musical resources to use music-*making* (as contrasted with music-*listening*) as a means of attracting new people and linking them with the fellowship before the point of commitment. Our pattern has militated against us using music-making for evangelistic purposes. But let it be confessed that since the dawn of music-*making* in the Army, enterprising leaders have 'assimilated' into their learners' classes and practices potential converts and potential soldiers and have by that means made the band and songsters vehicles of assimilation. They have worked to the Priority Principle.

The YP corps. The YP corps is a series of groups within a group. Each has its own significance and its own potential for assimilation and nurture, and they are only grouped together for reasons of space. The YP workers themselves form a group—and it is important that the group should remain absorbent and not become resistant. The way in for many PALS has been through giving a helping hand in the YP corps. The Sunday-school—ranging from the cradle roll, through the primary and juniors right to the teenage and adult classes—represents a high EP through both personal and corps links. The junior soldiers, YP band, singing company, timbrels are each cohesive groups with immense assimilative potential for other young people. Other groups like guides, brownies, scouts, cubs, SABAC, junior clubs and joy hours also represent Christian service and potential for evangelism of Presence, Proclamation and Persuasion. YP activities can.so easily become ends in themselves, rather than a means to an end. The Priority Principle needs constant re-emphasis.

The Army has always recognised the importance of reaching out to the young and attempting to fold them into the fellowship of the corps. More resources are devoted to that form of evangelism, territorially, divisionally and locally, than to any other. The young are highly receptive and the immediate response can be most encouraging. The impact of the Christian teaching and influence received cannot be measured. But when it comes to nurturing the young through to adult commitment as soldier disciples it requires a high level of commitment from leaders, and even then the yield is often disappointingly small. How to hold the young, into whom so much love, dedication and skill have been poured, while they cross the stormy straits of their teenage years, is a challenge not only for the YP corps but for the corps as a whole.

Corps cadets. The corps cadets are the all-important link between junior and senior soldiership. Technically they are a closed group, but leaders have always seen the potential for using the group and its activities as a means of assimilating young people on the fringe of the corps. If Christian nurture is to be effective it must include more than fellowship, and the corps cadet brigade is the chief agency for disseminating teaching about the Christian life, evangelism and all that is included in salvationism to the next generation of salvationists. Here again the Priority Principle needs to have its rightful place.

Recruits' class. Once the wheels of incorporating new converts into the life of the corps begin to turn in earnest, the recruits' class becomes the live centre of the corps. Whether known by its traditional title or a title like 'New Christians' group, this gathering is likely to be the most inspiring and heartwarming of the week. The team of instructors must obviously expand in line with the demand. The recruits' class can be open to unconverted people as well. Often the very process of learning what the committed Christian life is all about leads to the moment of personal acceptance of Christ. The recruits' class has remarkable potential for assimilation and nurture.

House groups. As previously mentioned, the lowly cottage meeting is now seen as the very cutting edge of evangelism in the modern society. A number of corps have house fellowships and they fulfil a valuable function in nurturing the spiritual development of the group members. Their potential for assimilation depends on whether they have remained absorbent to new people. The barrier of crossing someone's threshold has to be reckoned with.

However, it is in the realm of house groups *specifically designed for continuous evangelism* that the most exciting potential for growth lies. The group dynamics in such a fellowship are quite different. The group is a task force with a specific aim, and it is prepared to work towards that aim and then divide and divide again, like so many cells, as new people are added who themselves become part of the multiplying task forces. There are no set patterns. Some groups specialise in Bible studies specially designed for evangelistic use, some rely on speakers, others on guided conversation, yet others on discussions prompted by video presentations. As this is now one of the most alive arenas of evangelism much helpful literature and teaching material in printed and video form is available. The previously quoted *Small Group Evangelism* by Richard Peace (Scripture Union) is an example.

The corps that wants to grow needs to look carefully at the challenge of evangelistic house groups. In the present time there is no more effective method of cultivating, assimilating, nurturing and leading the receptive to Christ. Its starting point is the relational circles of those involved—and up to 90 per cent of new Christians took the first step towards Christ through such a relational circle.

Service to the community. Under this heading are grouped activities such as the league of mercy, luncheon clubs, play groups, charity shops, coffee mornings, and all the variety of forms that service to the community takes. Service is an end in itself. We serve because Christ served. But community service has also a double evangelistic potential. Firstly, by meeting the physical, social and emotional needs of people in Christ's name, we proclaim the good news of God's love to them. Some of them may respond spiritually to the gospel. But secondly, community service is one of the best ways we have of assimilating into corps life the many fine people in the community who are looking for ways of expressing themselves in Christian service. Newspaper adverts at Christmas time for helpers needed for corps Christmas meals usually elicit a surprising response. There is a vast pool of goodwill out there. And because of The Salvation Army's high reputation in social service it is readily tapped. It is a matter of identifying those receptive individuals and of cultivating, assimilating and nurturing them in Christ.

Other open groups. Other open groups such as drama groups, assorted fellowships, social occasions, musicals, youth and other choruses, have a particular value because of their openness. More or less anyone can belong! One of the secrets of growing churches and corps is that they have had the flexibility to create groups and activities that match the needs of the people they have targeted to reach. Groups need not have a permanent life. Some serve their purpose and should then be allowed to fade. A drama group is a case in point. It might stay together for a year preparing for a major event and during that time may be influential in the lives of many. But after the cycle of performances, it is perhaps right that its place should be taken by some other group.

The creation of *new* groups with *new* leaders and *new* people is fundamental to a growth strategy. Such groups provide outlets for new and emerging leadership and members tend to be possibility thinkers who, because they don't yet know it can't be done, go on and do it! Their only dictum needs to be Schuller's already quoted words: *the secret of success is to find a need and fill it.* New groups are dynamic and exciting, and if the Priority

Principle is kept in view, marvellous agencies of assimilation. Open groups of this kind may also spearhead evangelical outreach by experimenting with new methods, such as those listed under 'Other ways of looking at evangelism' in chapter 4 of this book.

Task teams. There are other groups of people in the corps who even though they don't come together for a meeting nevertheless form a group because of the common task they share. Such groupings include the heralds—*War Cry* sellers—and open-air meeting workers, carolling collectors, annual appeal collectors, sale of work team members, welcome sergeants, takers-up of collections, etc. These tasks have often proved very useful for the purpose of assimilating newcomers as every salvationist will know from experience or observation. They should not be overlooked when planning the over-all assimilation strategy for the corps.

If these then are the main constituent groups that make up a corps, what is to be said about the corps when it comes together as a whole?

ASSIMILATION AND NURTURE THROUGH CORPS EVENTS

The focal point, the climax of the life of the corps, is when it comes together to worship and for the proclamation of the gospel on Sundays. It is in the Sunday meetings that the groups join into one fellowship and the corps becomes a corps. Some groups may not be so well represented because their membership is not yet committed. That is to be expected. But every group needs to find its focus in the Sunday worship. Peter Wagner calls these occasions 'Celebration', and although we have reserved that word for inter-corps events, the Sunday meetings need to be in the nature of celebrations—whatever the size of the congregation. No effort ought to be spared, no method overlooked, no investment in equipment and publicity denied, no time in preparation begrudged to make the Sunday meetings the summits of the week, the apex at which all group activities meet.

Three points need to be made, each of such importance as to merit the status of a growth principle.

1. The Inspirational Meetings Principle

The 19th principle, the Inspirational Meetings Principle states: *To grow, a corps needs to focus all its resources on making the Sunday meetings the inspirational high point of the week.* Everything else needs to be seen as working towards and preparing for these crucial times of worship, teaching, challenge and decision. Every aspect needs continual review so that the appeal of freshness and relevance is not lost. As a step of faith the meetings need to be planned as if new people will be present. That might affect the choice of songs, the choice of items, the style of testimonies and other participatory speaking, the nature and manner of presentation of the message. Everything needs to be tested and evaluated and seen as through the eyes of a non-salvationist.

Radical decisions may have to be taken. There is a price to be paid for growth. Take the following practical issue as an example. Church growth research among *un-churched* people in some areas indicates that should they ever want to go to church they would want to do so *late Sunday morning.* Not early Sunday morning—for they like their lie-in—nor Sunday evening for that is not associated with church in their thinking. The Army programme has kept to the Victorian church pattern of 'saints in the morning and sinners at night'. But does that have to be reviewed? In a sense there has already been a move towards 'family service' type meetings in the morning, but would a corps be prepared to pay the price of gearing its morning meeting to outsiders if that were the only time they would come?

And what about the trend of moving morning meetings forward so that the open-air meetings—held *after* the indoor meeting—will not find people in bed? That is an excellent arrangement for the open-air meeting, but by the same rationale virtually eliminates the possibility of newcomers coming to a Sunday morning meeting indoors, for they would still be in bed! If in a particular locality community research were to confirm overwhelmingly the popularity of late Sunday mornings as the best time to attract unconverted people, that corps would reach a crucible of decision. Just about every opposing view would surface and just about every growth principle would be at stake.

2. The Bible-base Principle

The Bible-base Principle, the 20th on our list, states: *To grow, a corps needs to ensure that its life and worship are Bible-based.* Church growth thinking insists that it is neither coincidental nor accidental that it is the churches that are most firmly Bible-based that are the growing ones. The Army has a tradition of presenting scriptural truths in a down-to-earth and relevant manner. People are attracted to those who have found the answers, not to those who are still looking. Dr Roy Pointer includes some strong words in *How do Churches Grow?* (MARC Europe) about the effect a too liberal approach to the Bible has had on some. 'Many have become hesitant about preaching the gospel, uncertain about teaching traditional and basic Christian truths, reactionary towards their evangelical heritage, and disparaging of the supernatural in Christian faith and experience.'

But Dr Pointer also adds a necessary word of caution. 'The Bible is not merely the tool of men but an instrument of the Holy Spirit. Therefore an openness to the Holy Spirit is essential for all who seek to understand and communicate the word of God. The simple rhyme conveys the truth:

The word without the Spirit—you dry up!
The Spirit without the word—you blow up!
The Spirit and the word—you grow up!'

3. The Bring to Decision Principle

The 21st principle is the Bring to Decision Principle. *To grow, a corps needs to stress continually the need for the uncommitted to reach a point of decision.* Church growth thinking rightly says, not 'decisions' but 'disciples', and we know that our evangelistic aim is not only decisions but the making of soldier-disciples. But deciding for Christ is a necessary step in the journey towards discipleship, and much evangelism can be criticised for not even attempting to persuade people to take that initial step. Without decisions there will be no disciples!

Salvation Army meetings point traditionally to the mercy seat appeal at the end. It is right that they should do so. Obviously the appeal has lost some of its relevance where it is the same people attending Sunday after Sunday, but it will take on a new meaning when there are unconverted people present. A growing corps is centred on the mercy seat. Not only the mercy seat in the hall, however, for the salvationist firmly believes that people can be led to Christ anywhere. So whether it be on the street, in a home, in a group meeting or in the course of some other activity, does not matter, as long as people are finding Christ. A growing corps stresses continually the need for the unconverted to reach a point of decision.

These three principles should be foundational in the preparation for the Sunday climax of each week. But in closing this section, let it also be mentioned that there are times in the year, particularly at the seasons of the great Christian festivals, when the corps ought to seek to make the 'special' day even more special by arranging a truly 'big event' which by its nature will attract the unconverted. And that could also happen on a weekday. The day of the 'campaign' as such is by no means over.

ASSIMILATION AND NURTURE THROUGH CELEBRATION EVENTS

The arranging of inter-corps, divisional, territorial and international celebration events takes this book beyond its scope. But the Army's traditional emphasis on such united gatherings is founded on firm church growth principles. Christians need to get together from time to time in large numbers. The stimulus and inspiration of such events—not to mention their potential for evangelism—are now recognised as crucial to the growth of the individual units. Busing members and their contacts to large central gatherings is a recognised and most successful method of evangelism in many churches. Celebration events are not a luxury. They are a necessity. But it is only by the active support of the individual units that they can succeed in their inspirational and evangelistic mission.

This completes our survey of what it means to fold in new people within the corps. But who will do it?

For discussion

1. Discuss the Multiple Entry Point Principle in relation to the corps, and suggest any action steps necessary.

2. Discuss the Multiple Holding Point Principle in relation to the corps, and suggest any action steps necessary.

3. Does the corps meet the needs (a) of those who attend, and (b) of the people around it? Are there action steps that could be taken?

4. How successful is the corps at assimilating and nurturing, (a) through group events, and, (b) through corps events? Are there action steps that ought to be taken?

7
Mobilising for growth

It takes people to bring people. A picture of growth possibilities has been building up. But who will make it happen? The census board? Yes. The corps council? Yes. The leaders of existing sections, activities, meetings and groups? Yes. But beyond that? As mentioned, it will probably be necessary to form a growth task force—usually from within the corps council—and sub-groups to work on the statement of purpose, to analyse the present position of the corps, and to study the community. Immense work will have to be done by a 'caring group' to compile a prospect list and ensure that a whole network of carers reach out to the receptive. Some will need to ensure that the right arrangements exist for assimilation, and keep personal contact with each newcomer, monitoring his or her assimilation, nurture, shepherding and progress toward the point of decision and then beyond to discipleship. Others will be needed to help in existing groups, or to open new evangelistic and nurture groups, or to arrange evangelistic events and to pray and have faith. Everyone without exception will have his or her own relational circles with their evangelistic potential. It takes people to bring people. Who is going to do it?

If this seems discouraging to the smaller corps it might be helpful to quote from a piece written by William Booth when the Army was in its infancy. He entitled it *How to*

Command a Salvation Army Corps, and his first point was GET ONE! 'Before you can manage a corps,' he said, 'You must get one. There are plenty of street-corners available in any part of this great city and throughout the land, where any salvationist may find an audience and get a band together.' That is starting with one only. But the first convert will represent 100 per cent growth—and if his EP is 100 or more, that is where the soldiers and local officers of tomorrow will be found. And few today stand absolutely alone.

Where the officer does stand alone he has no option but to set the evangelistic process in train personally. But his aim will be to surround himself with a fighting force as quickly as possible. 'The description of membership as soldiership means *that there is no room for passive membership,*' writes Phil Needham. 'Members can be passive or active; they may do no more than belong on the rolls. Soldiers cannot only belong; they are either fighting or maintaining readiness for battle—otherwise, they are not really soldiers.'

With the passing of the years, however, there has been a tendency for the fighting forces to become more passive. To change the imagery, gradually and almost imperceptibly the corps officer has begun to be seen as the shepherd of the sheep. The one whose task it is to keep the sheep happy, to make them lie down in pastures green and lead them the quiet waters by. This picture of the church is unscriptural, un-Army and impossible if growth is the aim.

In a chapter entitled 'Ban One Man Bands' Roy Pointer tells of inviting people to indicate how many hours they feel their minister should spend each week on activities such as: pastoral visitation, other forms of visitation, prayer and Bible study, meeting and sermon preparation, preaching and teaching, administration, counselling, evangelism and training others for evangelism, denominational responsibilities, community leadership, family relaxation, and planning. One man mapped out his minister's week very nicely—but then discovered that it exceeded 200 hours!

There is no way that everything can or should be left

to the officer. That would be a complete misunderstanding of how the church is meant to work as the Body of Christ, and a denial of the brilliant way in which that truth was rediscovered in the concept of an army of salvation. 'Get set in your mind the ungainsayable truth,' said William Booth to his officers, *that every soldier can do something.* Don't wait to see if he is "sound", or to ascertain if he "will stand". You cannot afford to wait. Indeed, you must not *wait* for soldiers to find out what they can do and offer themselves: *you* must make the discovery, and hunt them out of their retirement, and bring them to the front. They ought to be set to work whether they offer their services or not!' Fighting words! But their wisdom is confirmed by Roy Pointer's comment: 'Church growth studies from every continent and a great variety of cultures have confirmed a basic New Testament principle—that churches grow when they mobilise their total membership to the service of Christ.'

The so-called Pyramid Principle, number 22 in our list, needs to be noted at this point. The Pyramid Principle states that 'for a church to grow it must expand its base of organisation and ministry before it may add to the mass of its followers'. Just as a pyramid cannot be made larger without its base first being enlarged, so a growing church cannot hope to cope with new people until it expands the arrangements it has for welcoming, assimilating and nurturing them. Even as simple an adjustment as increasing the number of welcome sergeants is a step towards enlarging the base. The corps that plateau at the 100, 150 or 200 mark often do so by failing to expand the base so that further growth is possible. In Army terms the principle reads: *To grow, a corps needs continually to expand its base for assimilation and nurture ahead of new member intake.*

RESISTANCE TO MOBILISATION

Why is it that even in a church with such an activist name as The Salvation Army it is rare for the full membership to be mobilised for God? A number of suggested reasons could be given.

☐ Some cannot be actively mobilised because of age or infirmity. This is perfectly valid. But they are the great 'upholders of arms' through prayer, faith, financial support and interest—and thus in fact remain fully mobilised in spiritual activity.

☐ Some may have become nominal soldiers, soldiers in name only. Church growth research methods include a nominality scale from A to D, which is a reminder that nominality is by degrees. Sometimes spiritual renewal or the challenge of a new task can awake a sleeping soldier.

☐ Some may undervalue the corporate nature of the Christian faith. They think of the spiritual life as being something exclusively between them and God. They don't attempt to 'mix' with the other members of the body. Helping them to see the true nature of the Christian fellowship and how their particular contribution is needed for the building up of the whole can help to mobilise them for God.

☐ Some may feel that the corps has no clearly defined aims and in consequence no cohesive programme, and therefore have little interest in participating. To mobilise its forces a corps needs to be able to give clear answers to questions such as: What are we doing? Why are we doing it? When do we need to do it? How are we going to do it? Who are we doing it for? Who is going to do it? Where do we need to do it? The I CAN strategy does at least begin to answer some of these questions.

☐ Some may not be convinced of the relevance of the corps programme or of its chance of success, and therefore are not motivated for participation. No one wants to commit himself to failure! But some who feel this way might be the very leaders who will open new areas of evangelism for the corps if challenged.

☐ Some may never have been asked to assume responsibility, or have been discouraged from taking on leadership initiative, or have been excluded by the

111

established leadership from joining their number. Every corps ought to have, at least metaphorically if not literally, a 'Situations Vacant' board prominently displayed and constantly brought to the attention of everyone. The system whereby soldiers are expected to sit back passively until approached by the officer is quite wrong. It places far too much responsibility on an already very busy person. When offers for service are made they need to be accepted and encouragement given even if they are not used in exactly the channel suggested. There are limits to the number of bandmasters the corps can cope with! And the local leadership needs ever to be on guard lest, quite unconsciously, they themselves are becoming a 'resistant group'. Apprenticeship for new people should not be too long. Young salvationists should not have to wait until out of their twenties—or even out of their teens—to be given real responsibility. As a rule of thumb according to church growth thinking, in a healthy corps one out of every five leadership positions—local officers, census board and corps council members—should be held by someone who has joined the corps within the last two years.

☐ Some may fear that their willingness may be abused. Some corps find themselves trying to sustain a programme beyond their available manpower, and individuals fear being exploited. This needs to be tackled with common sense and understanding. They may have a point, and something may have to be done about it. There may also have to be an understanding that the particular task will be taken on for a set and limited period only.

☐ Some may never have been helped to discover their spiritual gifts and then been assigned to the appropriate ministry within the corps. All Christians are called to a ministry and are gifted for it. It is reckoned that 75 per cent of Christians simply do not know their gifts. They do not realise that potentially they are equipped for ministry, and that there is a task within the Body of Christ awaiting them.

Roy Pointer has commented that 'it is not possible to

discuss the role of the laity apart from the gifts of the Holy Spirit', and this will therefore form the subject of the next section. But the Mobilisation Principle (number 23) which is so central to growth must be stated: *To grow, a corps needs to mobilise its members to active service for Christ in accordance with their gifts.*

MOBILISING BY GIFTS

Church growth thinking lays great emphasis on the making available of latent resources through the release of gifts of the Spirit in the life of the individual believer. Here again church growth thinking has taken the Army right back to its roots, but in so doing it has given an even more compelling rationale for the full involvement of every salvationist. We are not only to be active in God's service because by accident of birth or through conversion we find ourselves in a church with a militant name and which has soldiers who are expected to fight; we are to be active in God's service because *every* Christian is expected to be so as a member of Christ's Body, gifted, equipped and commissioned for service.

What is a spiritual gift?

In *Your Spiritual Gifts Can Help Your Church Grow* (MARC Europe), Peter Wagner gives a helpful definition which is here set out in a way which gives added emphasis to each part of the definition:

A spiritual gift is
—a special ability
—given by the Holy Spirit
—to every member of the Body of Christ
—according to God's grace
—for use within the context of the Body.

New Testament teaching on gifts of the Spirit can be summarised in the following 10 propositions quoted in the

113

'Saved to Serve' church growth module issued by the Australia Southern Territory:

1. Every believer is a member of the Body of Christ, which is the Church
2. Every soldier of the corps has a ministry
3. Every member of the body needs every other member
4. Every soldier of the corps has at least one spiritual gift
5. No one gift is required of all soldiers or is given to all
6. No soldier can command God to provide a gift for him
7. No gift marks believers as uniquely spiritual or special
8. All gifts are to serve the body, its upbuilding and its service
9. All gifts represent supernatural levels of more common ministries
10. All gifts are to be exercised in humility, unity and love

What spiritual gifts are mentioned in the Bible?

There are five lists of gifts in the New Testament. The Romans list (Romans 12:6-8) is often identified as the primary gifts, as the seven gifts mentioned represent the essential types of ministry needed in any local church:

1. Prophesying, or proclaiming God's word
2. Serving, or helping
3. Teaching
4. Encouraging, or exhorting
5. Contributing to the needs of others, or giving
6. Leadership, or administration
7. Compassion, or showing mercy

The Ephesians list (Ephesians 4:11) names five offices or ministries which involve gifts for their functioning:

1. Apostles
2. Prophets
3. Evangelists
4. Pastors
5. Teachers

The Corinthians list (1 Corinthians 12:8-10) mentions nine more unusual gifts:

1. Ability to speak with wisdom
2. Ability to speak with knowledge
3. Faith (of the kind that moves mountains)
4. Gifts of healing
5. Miraculous powers
6. Prophecy
7. Ability to distinguish between spirits
8. Different kinds of tongues
9. Interpretation of tongues

The other two lists are, 1 Corinthians 12:28-30 and 1 Peter 4:9-11, where 'those able to help others', and 'those with gifts of administration' are mentioned, as are the gifts of hospitality, preaching and serving.

Nowhere is it suggested that these are complete lists. John Stott makes the point that 'no single gift occurs in all five lists. The arrangement seems almost haphazard, as if to draw attention to the fact that each is a limited selection from a much larger total.' 'For instance,' adds Eddie Gibbs, 'it seems that Paul made his selection in 1 Corinthians 12:8-10 because there was misunderstanding and malpractice in the church in Corinth over these particular ones.' These biblical lists must therefore be taken as starting points rather than end limits for the variety of gifts that God can bestow, and the 'gift-mix' he can give to individuals and corps as a whole. Music is a surprising omission from Paul's list, so is writing, so is YP work, and these days the Spirit would expect us to include gifts of radio and TV ministry, perhaps even computer programming!

Points to watch

Gift exaltation. This term describes the temptation to exalt or rank one gift above another. All gifts are needed in the Body of Christ, 'The eye cannot say to the hand, I don't need you,' and neither can there be first and second class Christians according to the gift they have received.

Gift projection. This is an even more insidious problem whereby we are tempted to project our particular gift on to everyone else and condemn them for not having it. Unless recognised for what it is it can become spiritual blackmail to the one receiving the projection, and a cause of bitterness to the one doing the projecting. For example, the person specially gifted and called by the Spirit to sell *The War Cry* in the pubs can sometimes not understand why everyone else does not share his feeling of calling, duty and even excitement about his task, and may consciously or unconsciously condemn those around him. His attitude may engender deep-seated feelings of guilt in others and bitterness within himself. All because of a failure to understand that God gives different gifts to different people.

Gift of tongues. Because of its unusual nature and the unscriptural teaching sometimes heard that possession of this gift—which these days manifests itself mostly as a prayer language—is an indication of special Christian maturity, there is a danger of the greater issue of growth through gifts being blown off course by the side issue of tongues. This must not be allowed to happen. Anything divisive is a hindrance to growth. The Army's position is clear. The gift of tongues is a gift like any other. Salvationists who have received this gift use it in their private devotions. It is not part of the accepted salvationist tradition for it to be exercised in meetings. It would not be consonant with the aims of a movement dedicated to making the message clear and plain. The Army, however, respects those churches which allow tongue speaking in meetings and thus afford opportunities for those who feel called to do so.

Points needing understanding

Gifts and natural talent. A sharp distinction is sometimes drawn between a spiritual gift and natural talent on the grounds that only a Christian can have gifts of the Spirit. This is difficult to sustain, however, and the word 'gift' needs to be understood in a wider sense which does not separate too rigidly God's work as Creator and Saviour. Paul was the undoubted possessor of the gift of leadership. But he also had it when he was Saul of Tarsus organising the persecution of the Christians. In that case God took hold of what was already there and by redirecting it and enhancing it made it a gift of the Spirit. But no doubt Paul also received other gifts which had not previously been present when he opened himself to the Holy Spirit.

It is not easy to lay down hard and fast rules on the matter. Sometimes a spiritual gift is the enhancing of a God-given ability given through grace. It is usual for the 'born organiser' to find that that is the natural gift which God wants to turn into a spiritual gift and use, but it is not necessarily so. Some Christians have found themselves being led in quite new and unexpected directions in their service. There must therefore always be a readiness to respond to God's surprises. Perhaps there are other, secondary areas of natural gifting that he wants to crown and use, or perhaps he wants to give a completely new gift. Total openness to the Spirit is the key.

Gift and role. There are certain ministries, activities, responsibilities which every Christian is expected to carry out in his role as a Christian, whatever his particular gift or cluster of gifts. It goes without saying that the 'fruit' of the Spirit—what a Christian *is*—is for *every* believer, but even with the 'gifts' of the Spirit—what a Christian *does*—there are roles which are inescapable to the believer. The corps officer may have a particular God-given gift for organisation, but cannot therefore opt out of pastoral and evangelistic work. They are part of his role as a Christian leader even though they may not be his God-given forte. Similarly no one must be tempted to say 'I don't have the gift of evangelist so I don't have to witness.' Speaking up for the Lord, however simply and even if couched in terms of an invitation to a meeting or a brief word of witness is part of every Christian's role. Other examples: no one should say 'I don't have the gift of hospitality so I don't have to be hospitable,' or 'I don't

117

have the gift of giving so I don't have to give!' Spiritual gifts must not become excuses for laziness or selfishness or self-centred service. But they do enable us to identify our forte in God's service—and we need therefore not worry or feel guilty if we are not as effective as others in areas which to them are their strength.

Hypothesis of the 10 per cent

Peter Wagner originated the 10 per cent hypothesis in church growth thinking. The hypothesis is based only on observation, but the church growth movement has had the opportunity of observing thousands of churches—and the hypothesis of the 10 per cent has stood the test well.

The hypothesis of the 10 per cent is simply that in the average church or corps of whatever size, only 10 per cent of members have the gift of evangelism. That is a startling piece of information for a number of reasons. Firstly, had William Booth followed through on his original idea of keeping back the evangelists only and sending the rest to join churches he would have sent 90 per cent away! Secondly, the picture of the average Army corps as being made up mainly of evangelists is, and has always been, quite false. Thirdly, it is high time the guilt feeling which the 90 per cent tend to have was got rid of. Paul R. Orjala of the Church of the Nazarene comments in *Get Ready to Grow:* 'Too long we have been heaping false guilt on ourselves by declaring or intimating that every Christian who is really Spirit-filled should be winning souls like a professional. Those of us who *can*, find it easy to criticise people who can't. However, *every* Christian has the *role* of witness—which on occasion results in people finding the Lord. Every Christian needs to volunteer for evangelism training to find out if he has the *gift* of evangelist, and if not, to help him better to fulfil his *role* of witness so that he knows how to lead someone to Christ when the occasion arises.'

The matter of false guilt is dealt with by Peter Wagner in an even more striking way: 'The 90 per cent who have gifts other than that of evangelist should not be allowed to feel guilty if they assume secondary roles in the

118

evangelistic process. This is where God intended them to be, or he would have given them the gift of evangelist. In some evangelical churches the guilt trip for not evangelising is so severe that when the 10 per cent do evangelise and bring new people into the church the converts are turned off by what they find. The general tone of the body, the negative self-image of the members, the gloom and defeatism that can be felt in the atmosphere of the church makes them think that everybody must have been baptised in vinegar!'

'Some have special ability in winning people to Christ, helping them to trust him as their Saviour' (Ephesians 4:11, *The Living Bible*). They are the evangelists. In every church but especially in The Salvation Army they are the most precious people we have. There are only 10 per cent of them, on average, in every corps. It is up to the 90 per cent to help identify them and then support, encourage and work with them. For it is when there is full mobilisation of the membership and the full spectrum of gifts of ministry are exercised that the evangelists can be most effective.

The hypothesis of the 10 per cent has a sobering corollary, however. It is estimated that, though on average 10 per cent have the gift of evangelism, only about 0.5 per cent are actually exercising it. That is the 9.5 per cent theory. Were we to stretch that a little in view of our built-in emphasis on evangelism and say that 2 per cent with the gift are exercising it—it would still leave us with only two active 'evangelists' in a corps of 100 soldiers!

The actual and potential evangelists in our midst are our most valuable commodity. If ever there was a group of people who needed encouragement to discover, develop and employ their gifts it is the 10 per cent—and it is partly to provide that kind of back-up that the 90 per cent are there!

How to discover your gifts

The Quakers speak of God giving us particular 'concerns', and it is our concerns that point the way to

119

our gifts. The person who has a strong concern for the outcasts of society and the needy is likely to discover that he has the gift of mercy. The one whose eye catches any newspaper account of spiritual healing and who wants to know more, hear more and read more about it, is likely to be the recipient or potential recipient of the gift of healing. The one who finds within himself a burning desire to share the good news with others may have the gift of exhortation (counselling) or the greatly to be prized gift of evangelism.

Peter Wagner has, however, given us five easily remembered steps which have been of great help to many in the discovery, development and deployment of their gifts. The explanatory comments are also based on his writings.

1. *Explore the possibilities.* Through personal study read the relevant Scripture passages, read some recommended books, seek to discover what spiritual gifts are, how they are used, and how they relate to each other. Explore the possibilities also with the help of others whose judgment and knowledge you trust, talk about them in a small group, speak to your corps officer.

2. *Experiment with as many gifts as possible.* Experiment first with what you perceive to be your strengths. Learn how each gift is used in ministry. Don't be afraid to fail. Are you an organiser, a speaker, an evangelist? It is as important to discover which gifts you do *not* have as to determine which ones you *do* have!

3. *Examine your feelings.* We should feel fulfilled when we are using our spiritual gifts. The psalmist speaks of *delighting* to do the will of God. It is a complete mistake to think that because something causes me misery it must be God's will for me! But feelings can be deceptive and they must not be the *sole* indicator of our gifts or lack of them.

4. *Evaluate your effectiveness.* Spiritual gifts are given by God in order to produce results for his Kingdom

according to his will. Honestly evaluate your effective-ness. Are you bearing fruit through your gift? If not perhaps you are not gifted in the way you think.

5. *Expect confirmation from the Body.* Spiritual gifts exist for the health of the Body and can be recognised by the people who make up the Body. Seek confirmation from people you trust. Small groups can be a great aid in this—particularly if they know each other very well. Confirmation should be honest, sincere and ongoing. Be an encourager yourself and help others to be confirmed in their giftedness also.

Seeking to find one's giftedness can lead to the discovery that officership or auxiliary captaincy ought to be the way. There is no particular gift-mix which is right for an officer. There is a great variety of mixes, and it is probable that the 10 per cent hypothesis is reflected across the officer strength as a whole. Many of the pastors of large growing churches do not have evangelism as their premier gift. It is as likely to be leadership or faith or prophecy, or perhaps the gifts of a pastor or administrator. They become superb soul-winners by having the gift of releasing and using the 10 per cent evangelist strength within the body in addition to their direct ministry. It is in that sense that *every* officer is called to be a soul-winner. Feelings about officership also need the confirmation of the body—this is what the candidates system is about—and it is both scriptural and helpful for the 'Body of Christ' sometimes to take the initiative and suggest to members that they have the gifts for full-time leadership.

Once discovered, spiritual gifts have to be developed and deployed. The quickest way of developing them is usually by using them! But this chapter cannot end without touching on the vital subject of training.

TRAINING THE MOBILISED

The 24th principle, the Training Principle, states: *To grow, a corps needs to train in accordance with their gifts those it has mobilised.*

Church growth has given strong emphasis to the need for training and developing of Christians in accordance with their gifts, and when it comes to denominational seminaries and training colleges for full-time service it has tossed something of a bombshell in their direction. 'Present seminaries,' writes Donald McGavran, 'are almost exclusively concerned with turning out caretaker ministers to look after existing congregations.' In some of the most rapidly developing areas of the world some denominations have stopped sending away their trainee ministers to seminaries, for by the process of 'lift' they have found that they can no longer communicate with their own when they return. Instead they are being trained locally in 'seminaries of the street'. The Salvation Army has always maintained a practical approach to the training of its officers and church growth thinking is reinforcing the need to train in accordance with gifts and with an emphasis on producing leaders who make things happen and who are equippers of God's people. The demands of officership are more challenging and exciting than ever.

Training for lay salvationists must be in the twin schools of theory and practice. The corps cadet system has got the formula right. How to increase the opportunities for theoretical and practical training in all aspects of salvationism, at territorial, divisional and local level is a matter of continuous concern. Much has already been done, much is being done, but it remains a vast field which is still only being touched at its outer fringes. Growing corps will want to explore the riches available by way of training courses and material on evangelism—Bible study, communications, visitation, pastoral counselling, spiritual growth, church growth, effective community service, etc, available on the market generally and also from Salvation Army sources. Now that the video age has dawned the possibilities are literally endless.

For discussion

1. What organisational structure by way of task forces,

working parties, etc, might be considered in order to promote corps growth?

2. What factors affect total mobilisation? Are there any practical steps that might be taken to remedy this?

3. What are the chief implications for the corps of 'mobilisation by gifts'?

4. What types of training are most needed and how can further opportunities for training be provided locally?

8
Pioneering for growth

Two short chapters bring this book to an end. But no survey of church growth would be complete without a look at the aspect of pioneering openings of new corps and outposts. Of the various methods mentioned under the heading of reaching out and folding in there is no other evangelistic method that is as successful in terms of making new soldier disciples as the opening of new corps and outposts.

This was the chief method used by The Salvation Army in its early days. To go from 30 stations to 1,006 corps, and from 36 evangelists to 2,260 officers, in just eight years, meant that *on average* two new corps were opened and five officers were commissioned *every week* during those years. Though we do not have the membership figure, it is simple to estimate by postulating, say, an average of 50 soldiers to each corps. The growth was certainly phenomenal, and the main evangelistic method was the opening of new centres.

Lyle E. Schaller summarises church growth thinking on the point in *Growing Plans* (Abingdon) when he says: 'The first priority in any denominational strategy should be on organising new congregations. There are two reasons behind this recommendation. First, the organisation of new congregations is the most effective single method of reaching people without any active church affiliation.

Second, as a group, newly-organised congregations have a more rapid rate of growth than any other type of church.'

We are here looking at the next type of growth. Having studied *internal* growth and looked at *expansion* growth at length, we are now turning to *extension* growth. In so doing we move into an area in which—apart from the opening of a house group on the corps district—it is necessary to have cleared any projected plans with divisional headquarters before any attempt at implementing them is set in train. The Pioneeering Principle (number 25) states: *To grow, a corps and the Army generally need to pioneer the opening of new outposts and corps.* The wording is slightly different from the usual style, for when it comes to new openings the initiative sometimes comes from a local source and sometimes from the denominational network.

It is quite right to include the corps in the formula, however, for like so many things in church growth, there is an unexpected twist. As a general rule it has been found that the churches or corps which have a deliberate policy of pioneering new openings by sending groups on a permanent or semi-permanent basis to get an opening going, have found that they have taken in more new members back at base than the ones they lost to the new opening. Pioneering creates a spirit of excitement not only in the group going out but also among those that are supporting them, and this is conducive to growth. One church has found it so exhilarating that as a matter of policy it reckons to plant a new church every year. And it is none the poorer for it—quite the contrary. Extension growth seems to bring expansion growth.

Methods for pioneering new openings

The mushrooming of the early Salvation Army was through *extension* growth, and extension growth that came from the grassroots. Each corps, once established, looked to see where it could next attack and pioneer a new centre. The divisional officers gave leadership to this upsurge, but the powerful, irresistible wave came from below. Apart from seeking to steer its strength in particular directions there was little they could do, or would have wished to do, to control it.

The salvationists' methods were simple. The object was to invade a town with colours flying and then to ATTRACT ATTENTION! Any means seems to have been acceptable as long as it succeeded in ATTRACTING ATTENTION! So extravagant were some of these entries that friends and foes alike feared the Army might be mistaken for a circus parade. In Danbury (USA) it was, for when a real circus parade rode into town in 1885 the local drunks mistakenly attacked it with a shower of rotten apples! Once attention had been gained, the salvationists were ready with the red hot gospel. This was always first preached in the open air. A small group of the invading band would then usually seek lodging there while the main force returned home. They would find a small hall to hire for a meeting next night. And another corps had been born! Some of course did not survive, but an amazing number did!

Needless to say, such methods would not work these days. But church planting is still going on at an ever-increasing rate. Research into it has become a major topic in church growth. Much has been learnt, especially about denominational strategies, but at the same time it has to be admitted that it is difficult to reduce what is often so spontaneous to a book of guidelines. For the purpose of this chapter we will briefly mention some of the types of initiatives that are taking place, dividing them according to whether the initiative is taken locally or is part of a denominational strategy. Often the two will intertwine.

Pioneering new openings—local initiatives

☐ *Relocation.* For various reasons a corps may decide to move its buildings or relocate itself in existing buildings elsewhere. This is mentioned for the sake of completeness, but hardly classifies as growth.

☐ *House groups.* In some instances house groups have

formed the basis for new churches especially when a good distance away from the home base.

☐ *Feeder-outposts*. Outposts come in many shapes, sizes and locations. They are often started in schools or similar premises. If they lie close to the base, they act as feeders to that unit, with new converts being urged to join the main church or corps.

☐ *Independent outposts*. Outposts of this type lie further afield geographically and could therefore potentially become corps in their own right. The million dollar questions are: (a) is the body strong enough in numbers, (b) can it finance a full-time officer? and (c) where will it be housed? The general experience seems to be that rented accommodation (if obtainable) is preferable at first. It enables the situation to be assessed without financial pressure. It leaves the leader and members free to concentrate on people rather than buildings. But at some point the matter of a permanent building would have to be tackled or the new opening would decline.

☐ *Salvationist in new area*. Some corps have been started because a salvationist moved to a new area and began meetings in his home. In time it became necessary to rent larger premises. Eventually it became a corps. In some denominations it is deliberate policy to *ask* certain members to move to a particular area for that specific purpose.

☐ *Missionaries*. The ideal number for a group of salvationists setting out to form a new corps in a neighbouring area is considered to be one or two! A corps that starts on that basis will be truly local—not just a clone of the home one. Such salvationists would visit enough homes until they had sufficient prospects for a home-based meeting, and then as needed, would move into larger premises.

☐ *Larger group of missionaries*. Perhaps the most usual form of opening new churches or corps is for a reasonably large group of people to depart with the encouragement, blessing and financial backing of the home group to pioneer a new opening. The advantage of this arrangement is that a new corps is formed virtually overnight. The disadvantage is that they can easily settle with what they have rather than seeing themselves as a small nucleus preparing for something much larger. Such larger groups of missionaries have sometimes been formed on an inter-corps scale.

☐ *Task forces.* Some churches specialise in task forces of members who commit themselves to support a new opening for a determined period, say one year, after which they return to base.

Pioneering new openings—territorial policy

Denominations as a whole have to define their strategy, often working with great imponderables. Do they take the plunge and invest in a site, build a hall and then send in a full-time leader? Do they send in a leader for 'soil testing' (another church growth term) and then decide whether to build or not? Do they rely on the 'tentmaker' approach—by which the pioneer earns his living while establishing a church? And where do they pioneer? Near to existing centres from whence support can be drawn? Or far away in needy areas, miles from the nearest centre? What has been the relative success of recent openings in towns, villages, new towns, council estates, suburbs or larger cities, inner cities? What special features might have contributed to the success or failure in each of these cases? What about property and finance and the shortage of full-time leaders? These are some of the complex factors that have to be considered, and as, for the Army they take this book outside its remit, the options will only be mentioned in passing for the sake of completeness:

☐ *Tentmaker.* A lay salvationist earns his living whilst establishing a corps.
☐ *Officer.* An officer is provided with a quarters and an allowance for a determined period. Such officers need to be in the extrovert entrepreneurial mould. In many churches it has been discovered that certain ministers have a particular gift for this kind of work. After some

years establishing a church in an area, they move on and start again somewhere else.

☐ *Relocation.* Occasionally two or three 'struggling' corps are brought together in one new area with a new building.

☐ *Other ways.* Some of the ways, or variations of them, surveyed under the heading of local initiative, are sometimes used with divisional and territorial input.

Sometimes the pioneers who go out will seek to open a house group—using the quarters as the base—and then gradually move into other homes. Sometimes they will pursue a deliberate fusion policy whereby a number of separate house fellowships are commenced which are then brought together to form the church or corps when a central meeting place becomes available. An interesting point mentioned in church growth research and which seems to reflect the Army's early days, is that women are often more successful than men at this type of work. Another is that continuing financial subsidy appears to hinder growth. It creates dependency. Financial independence gives the group impetus. A key issue still being discussed is whether it is best to start small and build up, or whether to start big from the beginning. The former is in the traditional manner, so let Lyle E. Schaller describe for interest the second way:

'An alternative approach has been to find a person-centred, extroverted, dynamic, aggressive, entrepreneurial minister and send that magnetic personality out with three instructions:

☐ First, spend six to 10 months meeting as many people as you can and building friendship ties with them. Concentrate your time and energy on people who do not have any active church relationship.

☐ Second, do not schedule your first worship service until you are confident that you will have at least 200 people in attendance.

☐ Third, expect that to be the smallest crowd that you will ever have for Sunday morning worship!'

The subject as a whole is a large one and can only be touched on in this chapter. But church growth is now able to provide a body of research to guide both local and denominational initiative. The most exciting prospects for growth lie in the field of new openings. And initiative for extension growth which comes from the grassroots will be twice as likely to succeed as anything which comes 'from above'—and, though it sounds incredible, is likely to lead to both internal and expansion growth locally at the same time.

For discussion

1. What are the implications of the Pioneering Principle for the corps?

9
Projecting for growth

Peter Wagner speaks of the 'awesome power of meeting goals'. He quotes Arthur Adams: 'Faith is the most important qualification of a leader. A commitment to something so strong that it shapes the leader's life is contagious.' 'The number one requirement of having real church growth—unlimited church growth,' says Pastor Paul Yonggi Cho, who has 500,000 members in his church, 'is to set goals.' Goal setting never ends. 'By all means,' adds Robert Schuller, 'set goals *beyond* your goals. And if there are obstacles in the way that would keep you from establishing larger goals, realise that these obstacles must be removed at any cost—or accept the fact that the seed of death and decay is already planted.'

Any corps that wants to grow must develop effective planning procedures. It must (a) face facts, (b) establish objectives, (c) set goals, (d) make plans, (e) assess results— all in a continuous cycle, not once and for all. But here we are dealing not so much with managerial matters as with the point where our objectives and our faith meet.

Our objectives might be set out in the statement of purpose for the corps (chapter 2) or will be generally known through all that The Salvation Army stands for. But our goals are the means whereby we intend to achieve those objectives. To be good goals they need to be:

☐ *Relevant goals*—consistent with the main purpose of

131

leading people to Christ and through to soldier discipleship.

☐ *Measurable goals*—set in time and quantity so that it will be known whether they are achieved or not. Something specific that can be measured, to be achieved before a set date.

☐ *Achievable goals*—not so high as to be impossible, but neither so low as to require no faith or action.

☐ *Significant goals*—significant enough to make a real difference. We can get in God's way if we think too small.

☐ *Personal goals*—goals that have the endorsement of the corps as a whole. They then become 'owned' goals and members are much more likely to pray and work for their fulfilment than with imposed goals.

We set goals because goals are a stimulus to life. They become faith projections. In setting goals we are determining as best we can the growth that we believe to be God's will, and then taking positive steps to provide for this growth. The idea has been summarised in five propositions:

1. Faithfulness to the Lord requires making disciples of all nations
2. Faith pleases God
3. Faith projections are realistic goals based on facts
4. Faith projections are a team effort set by those who will fulfil them
5. Through prayer we seek God's will as to our projections and receive his power to see them fulfilled.

Is it right to set such goals? Yes—God honours goal setting that is realistic and yet faith-provoking. Is it necessary? Yes—because without clear goals human nature tends to settle for very little, and the power of faith and expectancy is lost. Is it dangerous? Isn't failure a continual risk? Yes—but as long as the goals are group-owned the risk is not a problem. It will be up to the group to modify them if necessary. Perhaps they will turn out to have been too unrealistic in the first place.

The principle is sufficiently cardinal to be stated in the form of a set principle, number 26. The Faith Projection

Principle states: *To grow, a corps needs to have the courage to project by faith its goals and objectives for growth.*

Corps faith projections

A number of groups, including the corps council and possibly the whole body of soldiery, will need to be involved over a period of time in arriving at a Faith Projection for the corps as a whole, a projection which will be truly owned by the soldiers and not imposed upon them.

The corps Faith Projection may state a number of main objectives, especially to do with the number of new people it is hoped will be won, and may even refer to technical terms like the rate of composite growth. The Faith Projection may be for the year ahead or for the decade ahead.

Those global objectives will need to be broken down into specific goals and perhaps even action steps. What can be done now—and what next month—to help achieve our over-all objectives? Many of the matters that a book like this will have brought up for discussion will have to be considered carefully.

For example, it may be felt that the fellowship of the corps should have greater warmth and vitality in order to be more attractive to newcomers. How might that objective be achieved? The first short range goal could be for greater stress to be laid on the scriptural truth that we belong to the Body of Christ and are members of it. Action step: Corps officer to be asked whether a series of addresses on the subject could be planned. The second short range goal could be to have more soldiers participate in the meetings, lead testimony periods, speak about favourite songs, etc. Action step: Corps sergeant-major to be asked to draw up roster and follow through.

Human nature being what it is, it is reasonably easy to set goals in a flush of enthusiasm—but then to forget about them. Any system, if it is to work, must have built into it a way of monitoring progress. The corps council, subgroups of that council, annual or twice annual commitment/renewal weekends, soldiers' meetings, 'wind up' meetings on Sunday nights, are all possible occasions for report back to take place.

Group faith projections

But it is not only the corps as a whole that needs to take the step of faith and enter into a faith projection following prayer. Every group within the corps ought to see this as a permanent and recurring challenge. As each goal is reached, so the new ones should be beckoning on ahead. Group goals will have a tendency to become insular and it is vital that the Priority Principle be ever kept in view: *to grow, a corps—and each group within it—must make evangelism its priority.*

Finally

Our starting point was that to grow, a corps must believe that it can. Now that we have looked at some of the works that have to be added to our faith the challenge perhaps seems greater than ever. But the challenge cannot be evaded. It is hard to get round the simple truth that The Salvation Army exists to get people saved. And to get people saved is what church growth is all about.

For discussion

1. What are some of the goals and objectives that might be included in a draft of a Faith Projection for the corps?

2. What is the response of the corps to the challenge of church growth?

26 Key Growth Principles mentioned in the text

1. The Expectation Principle (page 14)
   To grow, a corps must believe that it can.

2. The Leadership Commitment Principle (page 21)
   To grow, the leadership of a corps must want it to grow and be prepared to pay the price.

3. The Corps Commitment Principle (page 24)
   To grow, the corps as a whole must want it to grow and be prepared to pay the price.

4. The Priority Principle (page 25)
   To grow, a corps—and each group within it—must make evangelism its priority.

5. The Prayer Principle (page 27)
   To grow, a corps must engage continuously in believing prayer for growth.

6. The Face Facts Principle (page 28)
   To grow, a corps needs to face the facts about itself with ruthless honesty.

7. The Balanced Work-force Principle (page 35)
   To grow, a corps needs to achieve the right balance between maintenance and outreach leaders/workers.

8. The Work from Strengths Principle (page 47)
   To grow, a corps needs to recognise and work from its strengths.

9. The Growth Strategy Principle (page 53)
   To grow, a corps needs to have a definite strategy for growth.

10. The Soldier-Disciple Principle (page 58)
    To grow, a corps must have as its evangelistic aim the making of soldier-disciples.

11. The Receptivity Principle (page 61)
    To grow, a corps must concentrate its evangelistic resources on those most receptive to the gospel.

12. The Pragmatic Principle (page 64)
    To grow, a corps must use the evangelistic methods most calculated to achieve the aim of making soldier-disciples.

13. The Personal Link Principle (page 71)
    To grow, a corps needs to reach out to those who are receptive through having personal links with members of the corps.

14. The Corps Link Principle (page 74)
    To grow, a corps needs to reach out to those who are receptive through having past or present links with the activities of the corps.

15. The Multiple Entry Point Principle (page 93)
    To grow, a corps needs to provide multiple entry points through its activities, meetings, groups and programmes in order to assimilate new people.

16. The Multiple Holding Point Principle (page 93)
    To grow, a corps needs to provide multiple holding points through its activities, meetings, groups and programmes in order to nurture, shepherd, train and use its new and existing people.

17. The Like Appreciates Like Principle (page 94)
    To grow, a corps needs to establish as many points in common as it can with the people it is trying to reach.

18. The Meet Needs Principle (page 95)
    To grow, a corps should seek to meet the needs of the people it is trying to reach and hold.

19. The Inspirational Meetings Principle (page 104)
    To grow, a corps needs to focus all its resources on making the Sunday meetings the inspirational high point of the week.

20. The Bible-base Principle (page 105)
    To grow, a corps needs to ensure that its life and worship are Bible-based.

21. The Bring to Decision Principle (page 106)
    To grow, a corps needs to stress continually the need for the uncommitted to reach a point of decision.

22. The Pyramid Principle (page 110)
    To grow, a corps needs continually to expand its base for assimilation and nurture ahead of new member intake.

23. The Mobilisation Principle (page 113)
    To grow, a corps needs to mobilise its members to active service for Christ in accordance with their gifts.

24. The Training Principle (page 121)
    To grow, a corps needs to train in accordance with their gifts those it has mobilised.

25. The Pioneering Principle (page 125)
    To grow, a corps and the Army generally need to pioneer the opening of new outposts and corps.

26. The Faith Projection Principle (page 132)
    To grow, a corps needs to have the courage to project by faith its goals and objectives for growth.

Selected bibliography

How do churches grow? by Roy Pointer (MARC Europe)

The Growth Book by Roy Pointer (MARC Europe)

I believe in church growth by Eddie Gibbs (Hodder & Stoughton)

Your spiritual gifts can help your church grow by C. Peter Wagner (MARC Europe)

Leading your church to growth by C. Peter Wagner (MARC Europe)

Church alive by Peter Cotterell (Inter-Varsity)